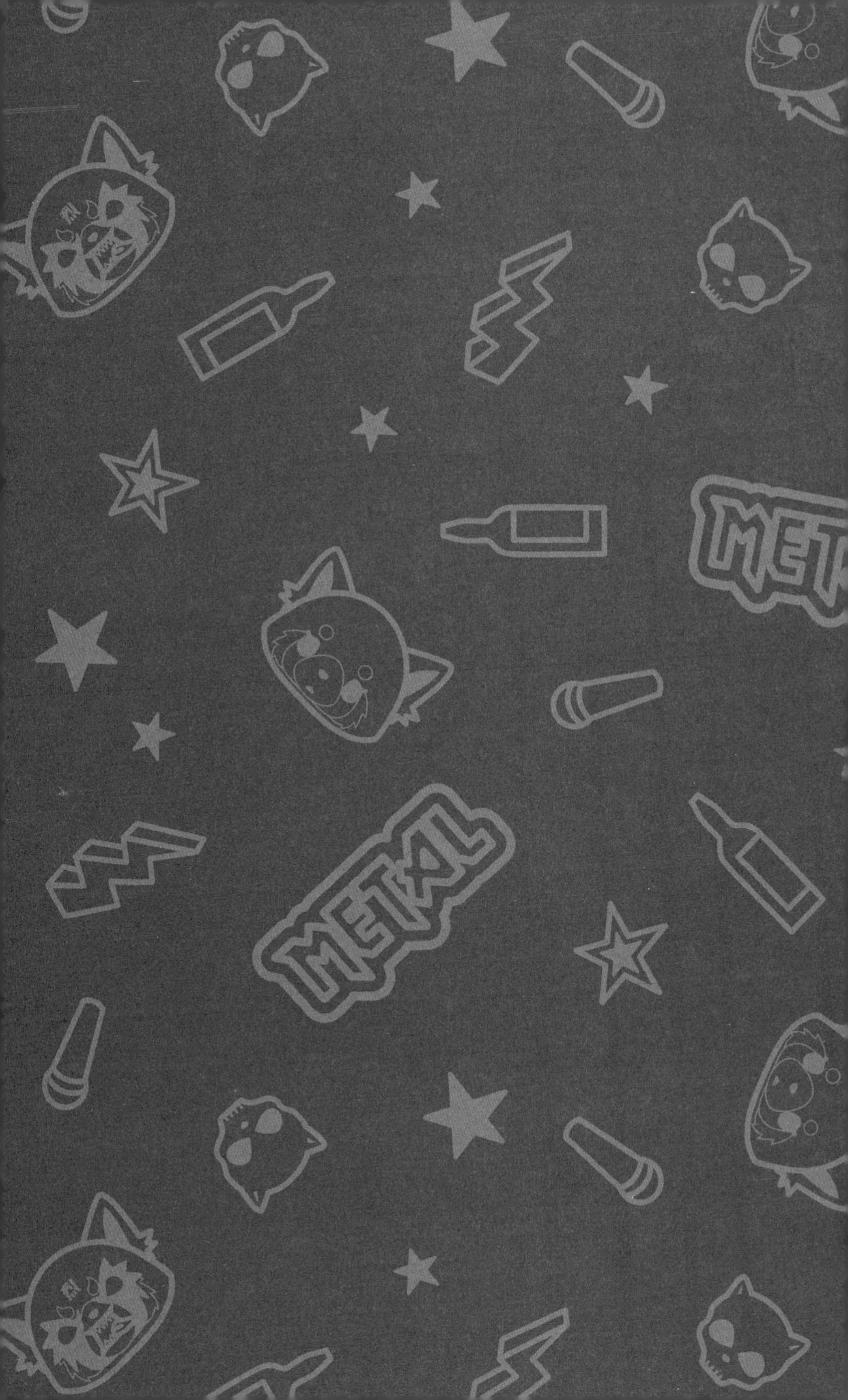
METAL

Aggretsuko™

STRESS MANAGEMENT

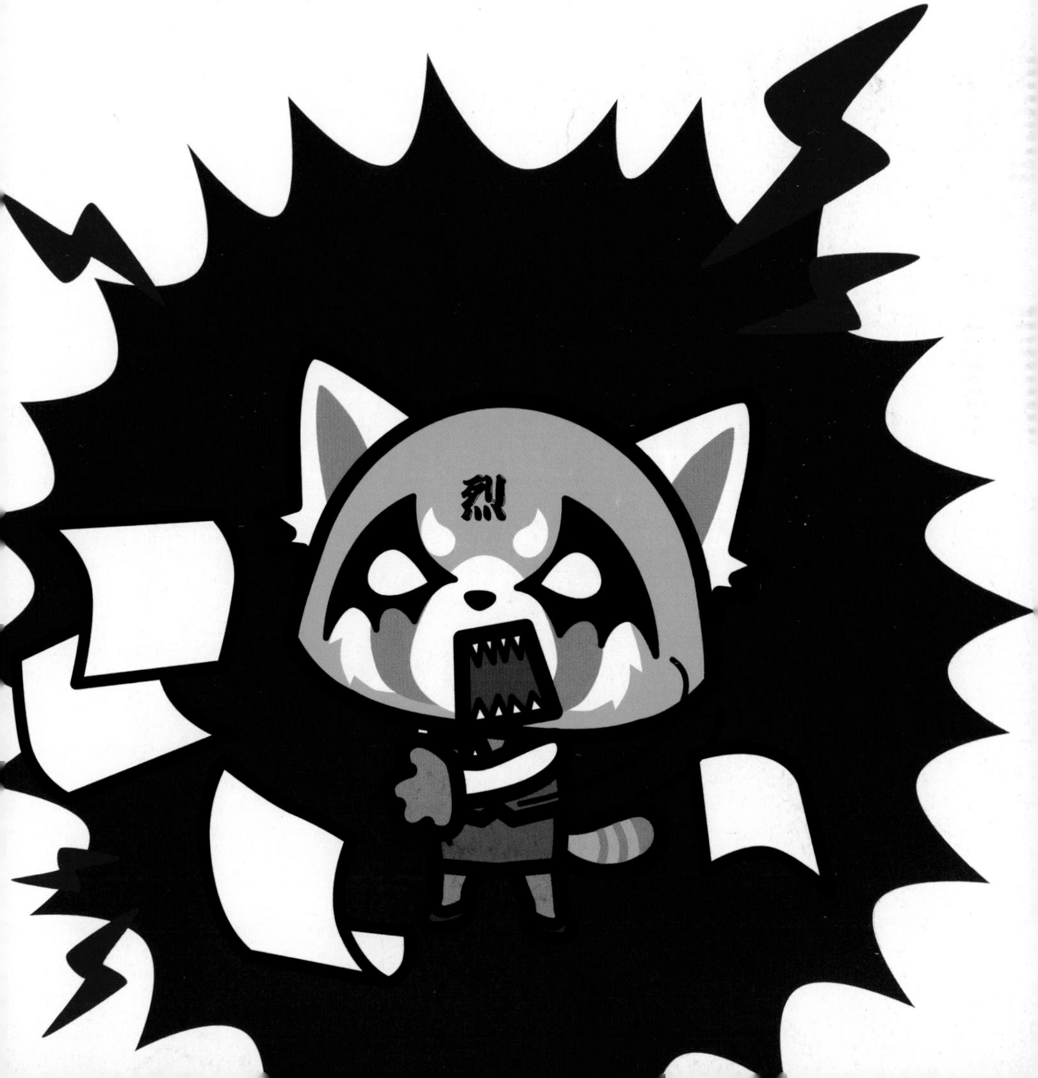
烈

MENTAL BREAKDOWN

WRITTEN BY Michelle Gish ILLUSTRATED BY Patabot
COLORS BY Sarah Stern

COLD SNAP

WRITTEN BY Sarah Stern ILLUSTRATED BY Shadia Amin
COLORS BY Sarah Stern

THE CARRIER CUP

WRITTEN BY Daniel Barnes ILLUSTRATED BY D.J. Kirkland
COLORS BY Andrew Dalhouse

ALL PAGES LETTERED BY Crank!
REGULAR COVER BY Patabot VARIANT COVER BY George Caltsoudas

Aggretsuko™

STRESS MANAGEMENT

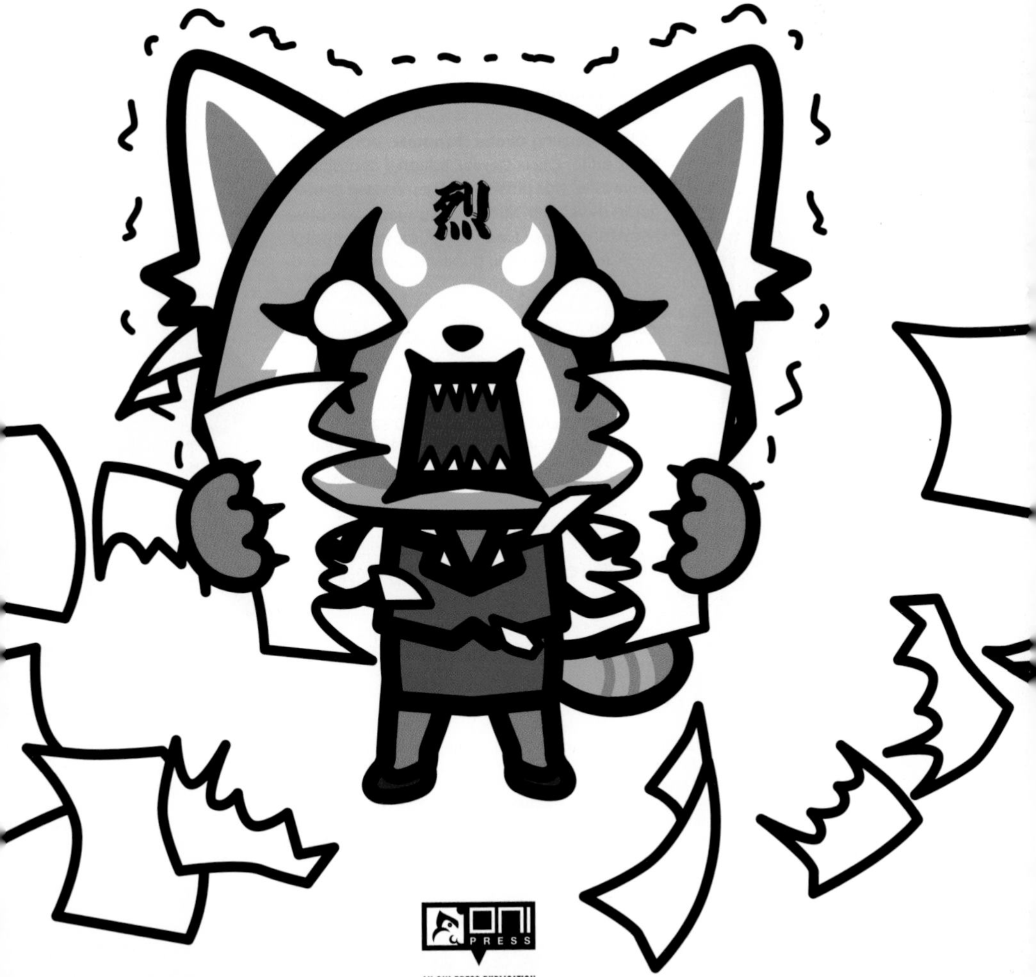
烈

ONI PRESS

AN ONI PRESS PUBLICATION

DESIGNED BY SARAH ROCKWELL   **EDITED BY** SARAH GAYDOS AND ROBERT MEYERS

SPECIAL THANKS TO
CINDY SUZUKI, JEFF PARKER, MARJORIE SANTOS,
SUZAN ZHANG, SUSAN TRAN, RENEE HAMMER,
ELLEN IZYKOWSKI, AND LINH FORSE
FOR THEIR INVALUABLE ASSISTANCE.

onipress.com

@onipress

lionforge.com

@lionforge

PUBLISHED BY ONI-LION FORGE PUBLISHING GROUP, LLC
James Lucas Jones, president & publisher
Sarah Gaydos, editor in chief **Charlie Chu**,
e.v.p. of creative & business development
Brad Rooks, director of operations **Amber
O'Neill**, special projects manager **Harris Fish**,
events manager **Margot Wood**, director of
marketing & sales **Devin Funches**, sales &
marketing manager **Katie Sainz**, marketing
manager **Tara Lehmann**, publicist **Troy Look**,
director of design & production **Kate Z. Stone**,
senior graphic designer **Sonja Synak**, graphic
designer **Hilary Thompson**, graphic designer
Sarah Rockwell, junior graphic designer **Angie
Knowles**, digital prepress lead **Vincent Kukua**,
digital prepress technician **Jasmine Amiri**, senior
editor **Shawna Gore**, senior editor **Amanda
Meadows**, senior editor **Robert Meyers**, senior
editor, licensing **Grace Bornhoft**, editor **Zack
Soto**, editor **Chris Cerasi**, editorial coordinator
Steve Ellis, vice president of games **Ben Eisner**,
game developer **Michelle Nguyen**, executive
assistant **Jung Lee**, logistics coordinator
Joe Nozemack, publisher emeritus

sanrio.com

 @sanrio

 @aggretsuko

aggretsuko

 @aggretsuko

aggretsuko

©2015, 2020 SANRIO CO., LTD.
S/T·F
Used Under License.
www.sanrio.com

SIL-34865

First Edition: October 2020
REGULAR ISBN 978-1-62010-821-5
ONI EXCLUSIVE VARIANT ISBN 978-1-62010-835-2
eISBN 978-1-62010-829-1

Printing numbers:
1 3 5 7 9 10 8 6 4 2

Library of Congress Control Number 2020937764

Printed in USA.

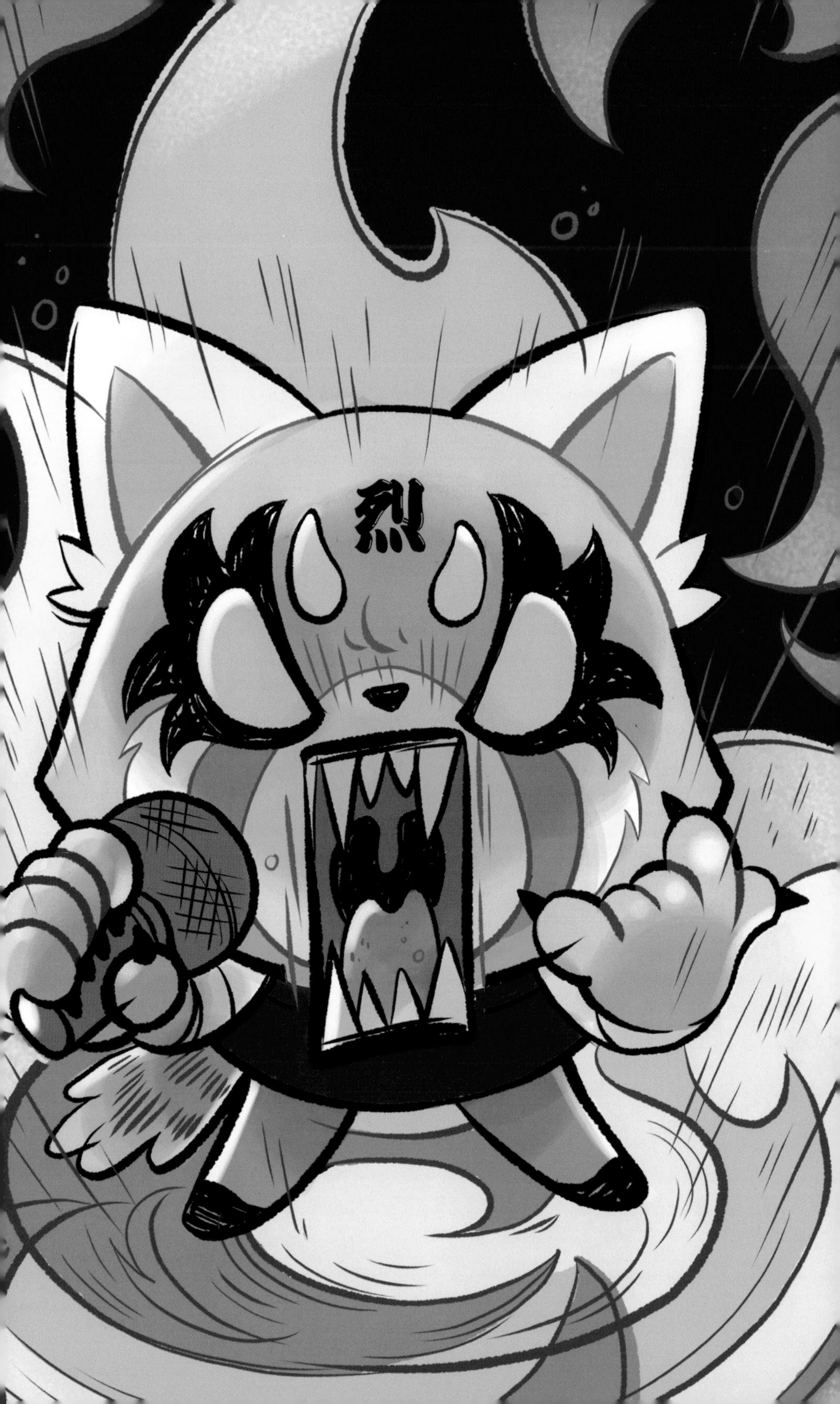
烈

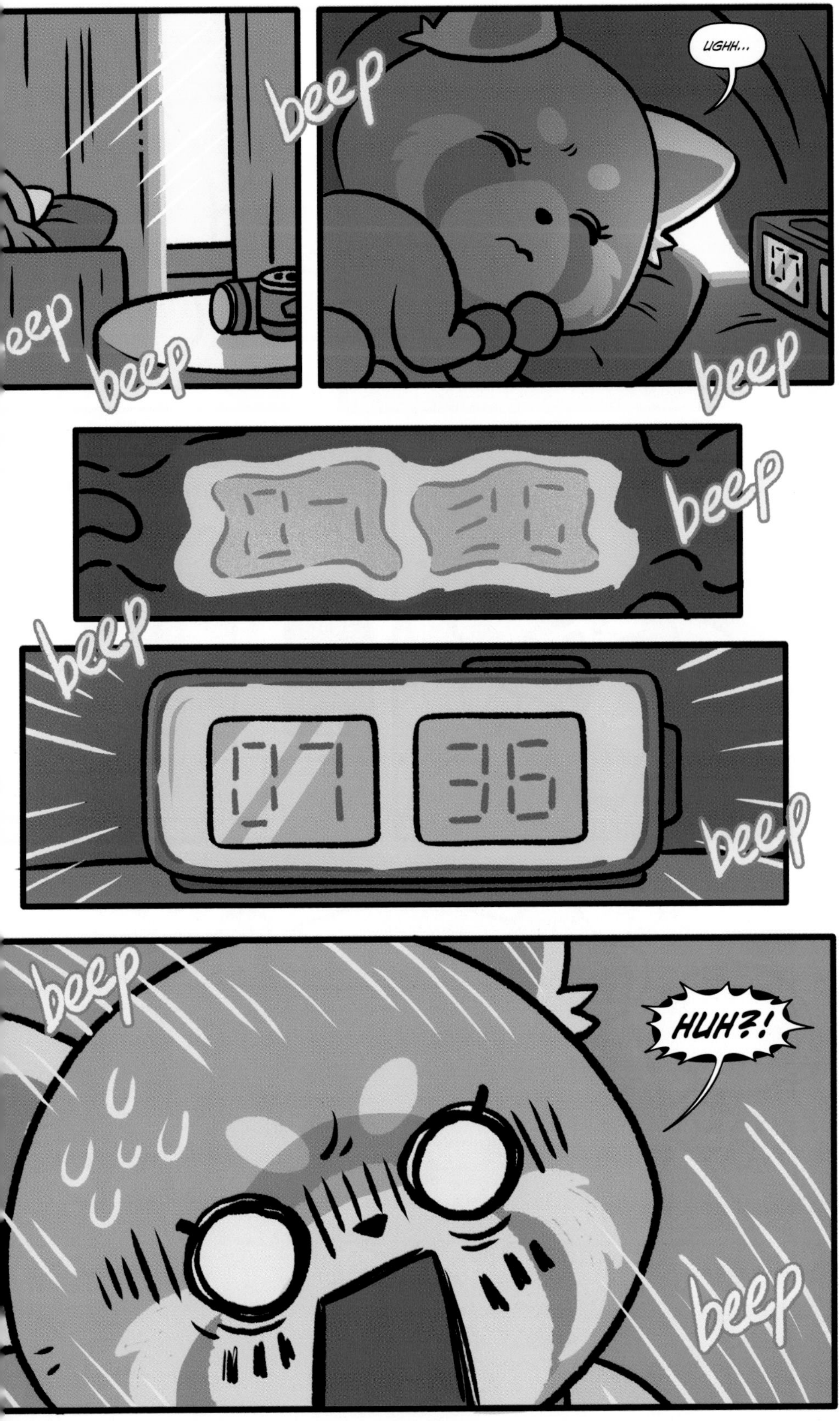
beep
eep
beep
UGHH...
beep
beep
beep
beep
beep
HUH?!
beep

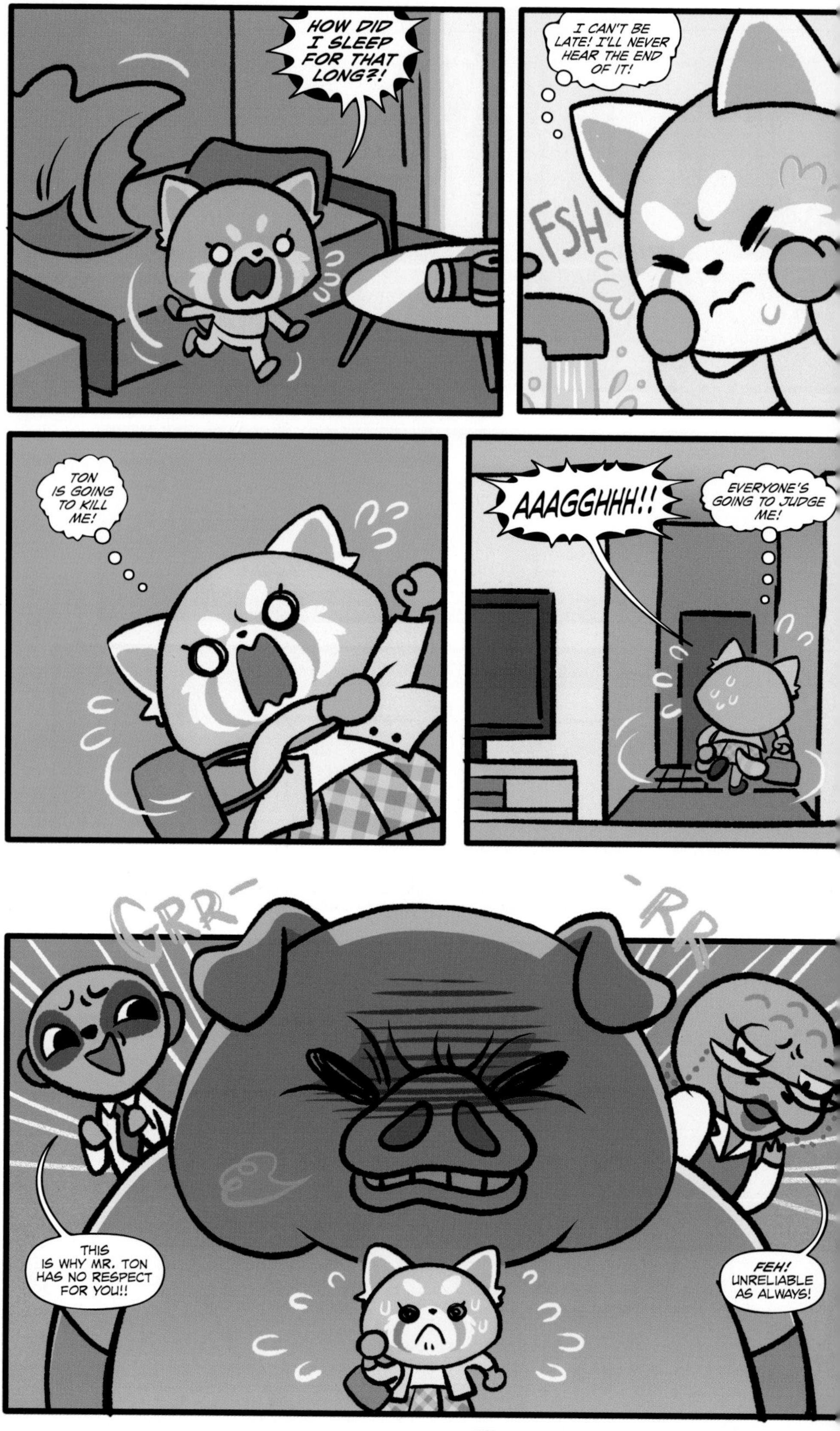
HOW DID I SLEEP FOR THAT LONG?!
I CAN'T BE LATE! I'LL NEVER HEAR THE END OF IT!
FSH
TON IS GOING TO KILL ME!
AAAGGHHH!!
EVERYONE'S GOING TO JUDGE ME!
GRR-
-RR
THIS IS WHY MR. TON HAS NO RESPECT FOR YOU!!
FEH! UNRELIABLE AS ALWAYS!

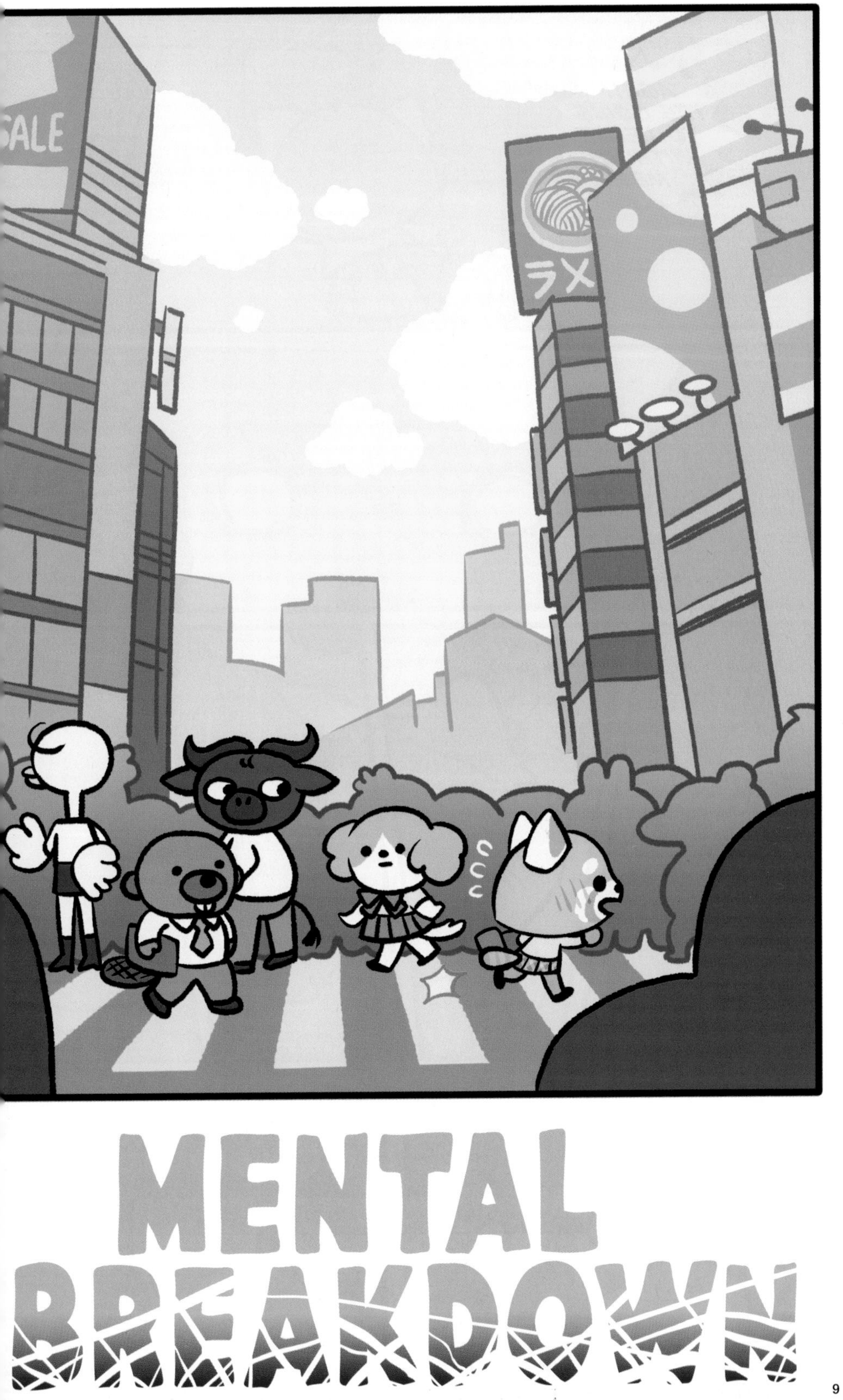

SALE
ラメ

MENTAL BREAKDOWN

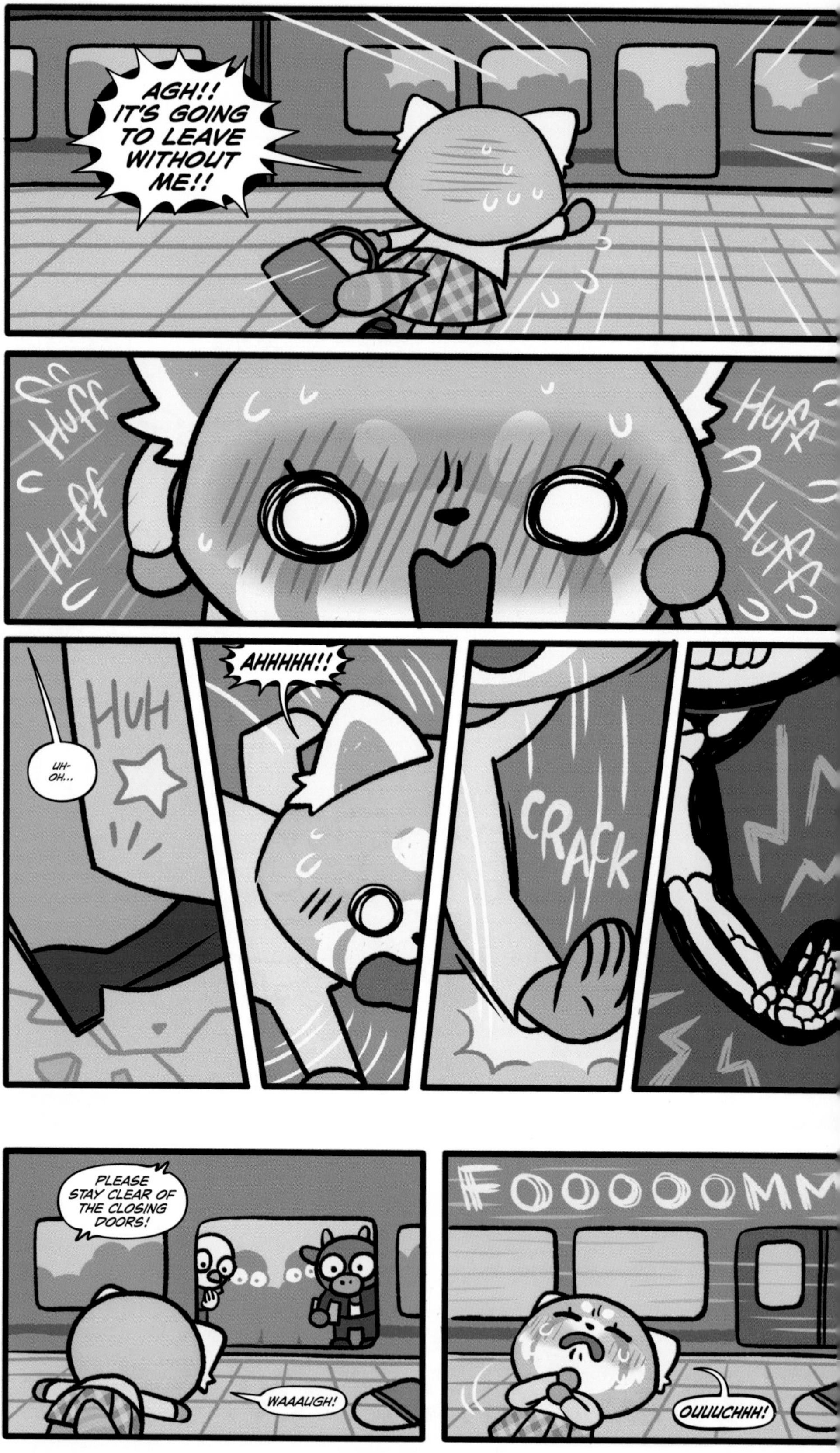
AGH!! IT'S GOING TO LEAVE WITHOUT ME!!
HUFF
HUFF
HUFF
HUFF
HUH
UH-OH...
AHHHHH!!
CRACK
PLEASE STAY CLEAR OF THE CLOSING DOORS!
WAAAUGH!
FOOOOOMM
OUUUCHHH!

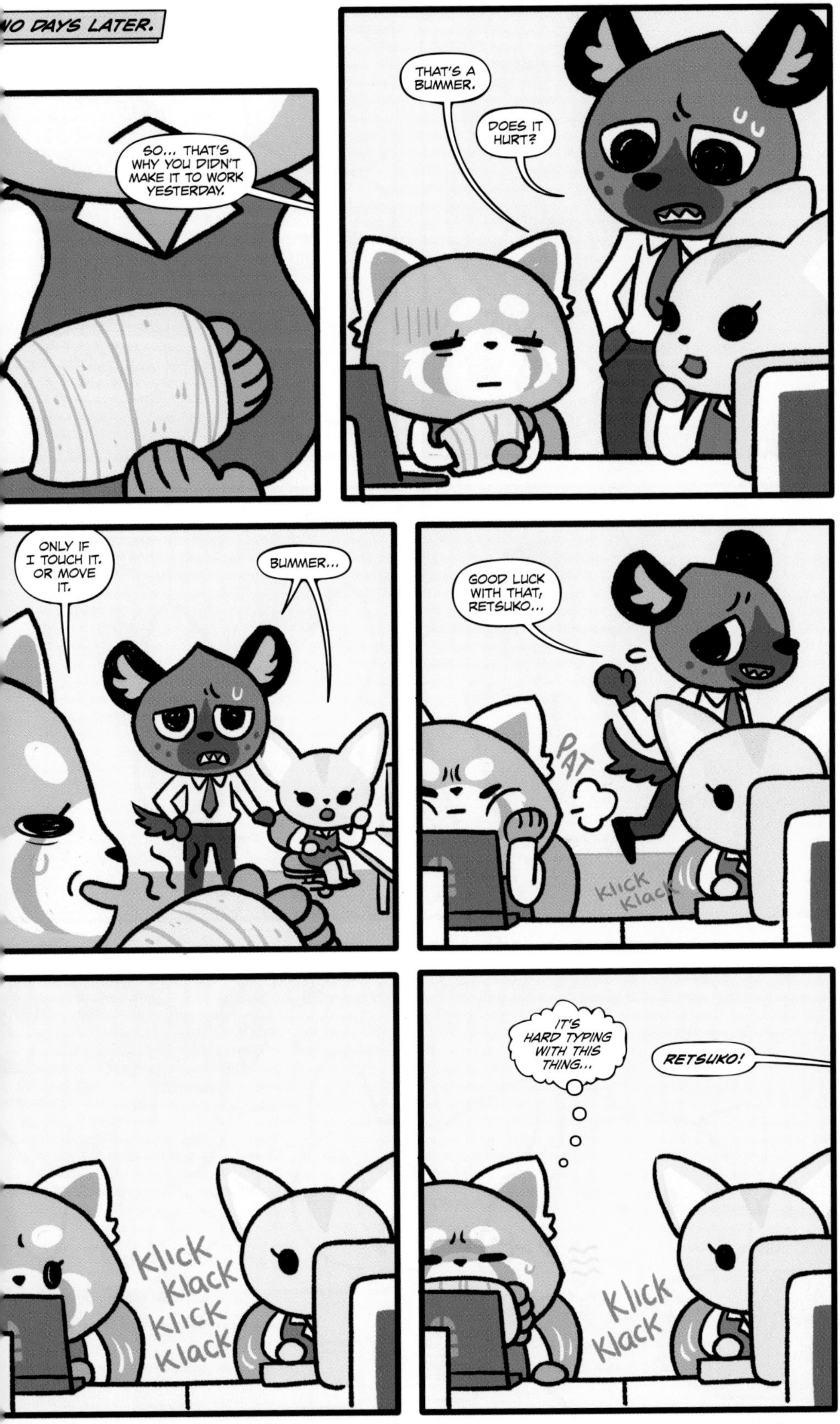

O DAYS LATER.
SO... THAT'S WHY YOU DIDN'T MAKE IT TO WORK YESTERDAY.
THAT'S A BUMMER.
DOES IT HURT?
ONLY IF I TOUCH IT. OR MOVE IT.
BUMMER...
GOOD LUCK WITH THAT, RETSUKO...
PAT
KLICK KLACK
KLICK KLACK KLICK KLACK
IT'S HARD TYPING WITH THIS THING...
RETSUKO!
KLICK KLACK

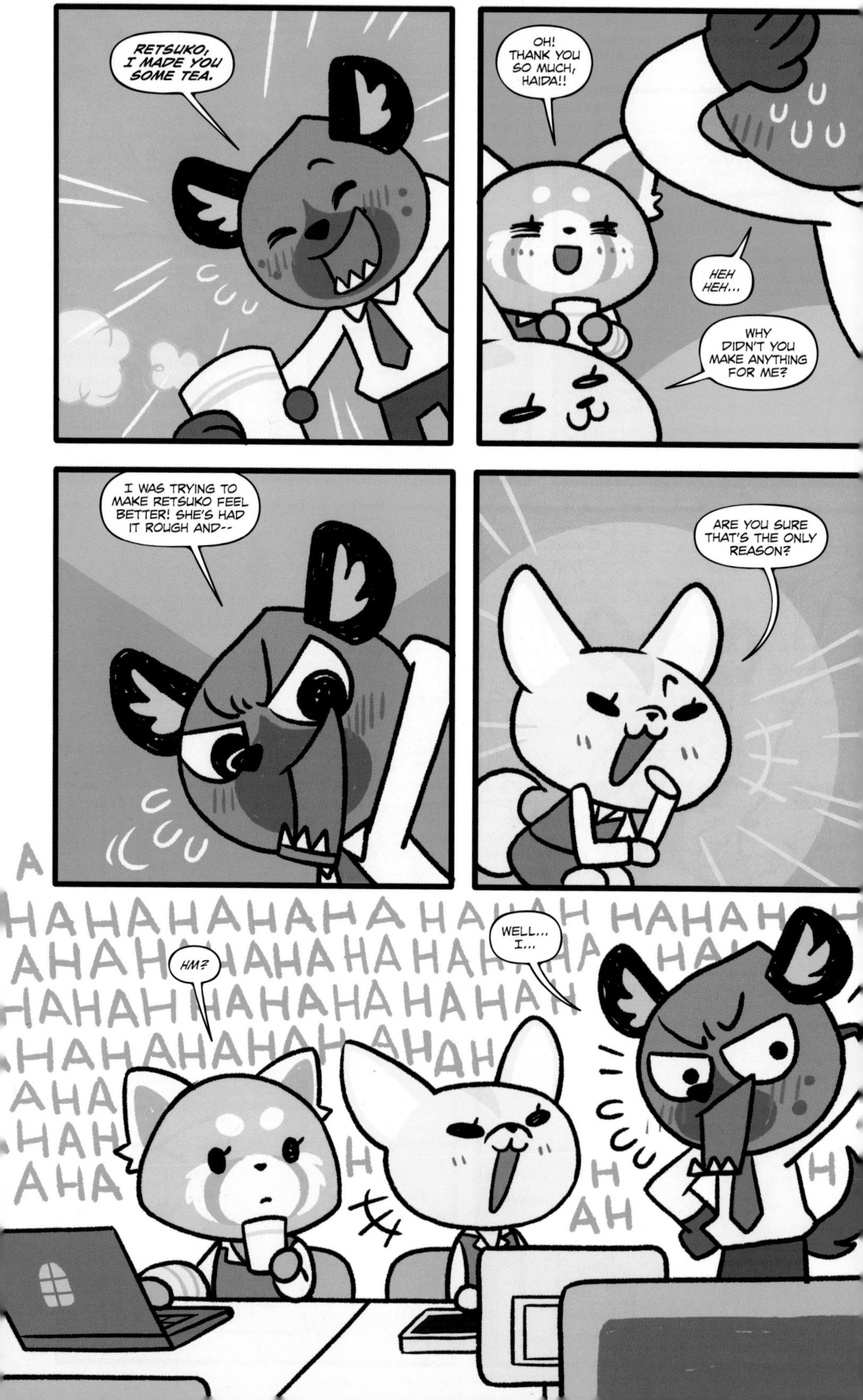
RETSUKO, I MADE YOU SOME TEA.
OH! THANK YOU SO MUCH, HAIDA!!
HEH HEH...
WHY DIDN'T YOU MAKE ANYTHING FOR ME?
I WAS TRYING TO MAKE RETSUKO FEEL BETTER! SHE'S HAD IT ROUGH AND--
ARE YOU SURE THAT'S THE ONLY REASON?
HM?
WELL... I...

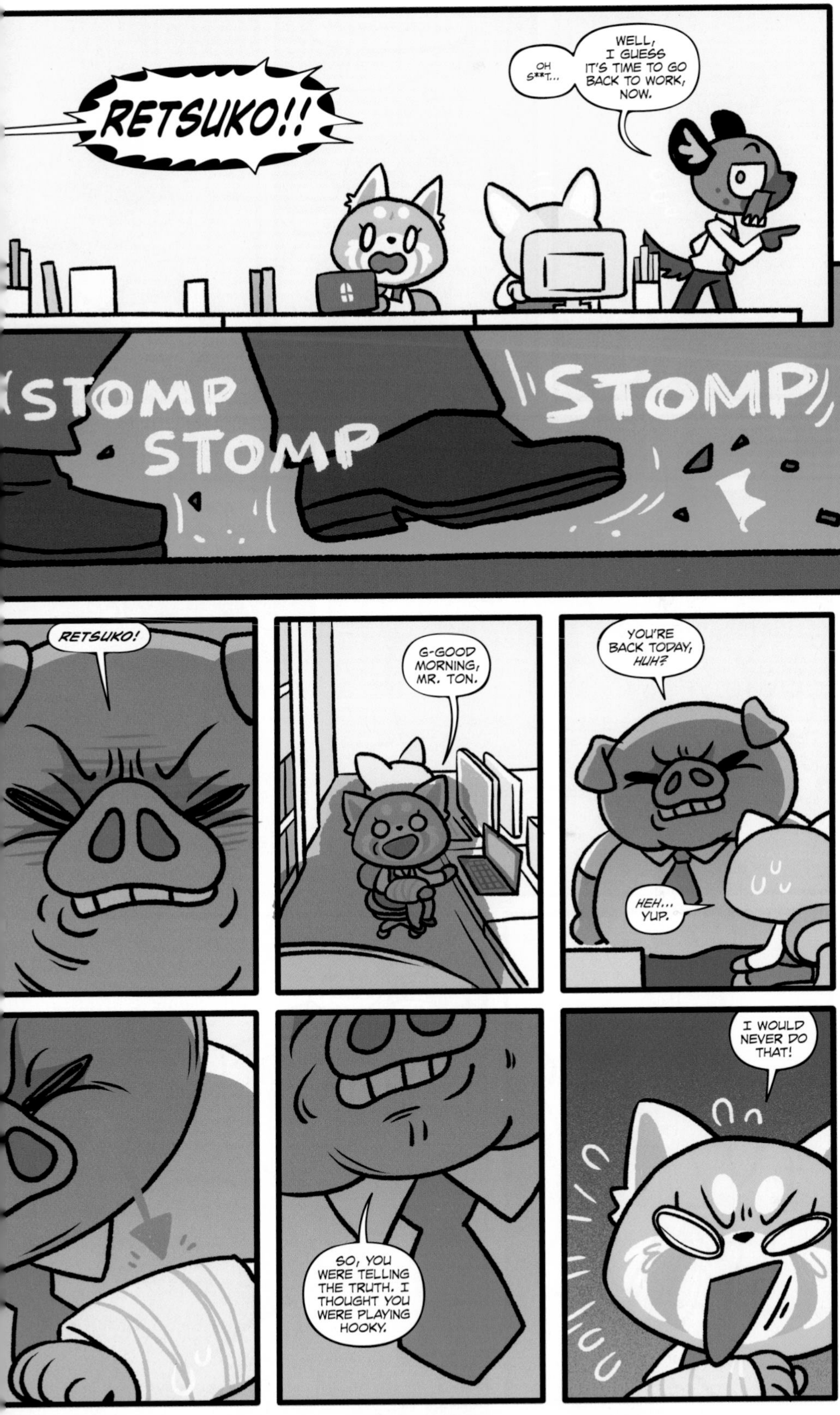
RETSUKO!!
OH S**T...
WELL, I GUESS IT'S TIME TO GO BACK TO WORK, NOW.
STOMP
STOMP
STOMP
RETSUKO!
G-GOOD MORNING, MR. TON.
YOU'RE BACK TODAY, HUH?
HEH... YUP.
SO, YOU WERE TELLING THE TRUTH. I THOUGHT YOU WERE PLAYING HOOKY.
I WOULD NEVER DO THAT!

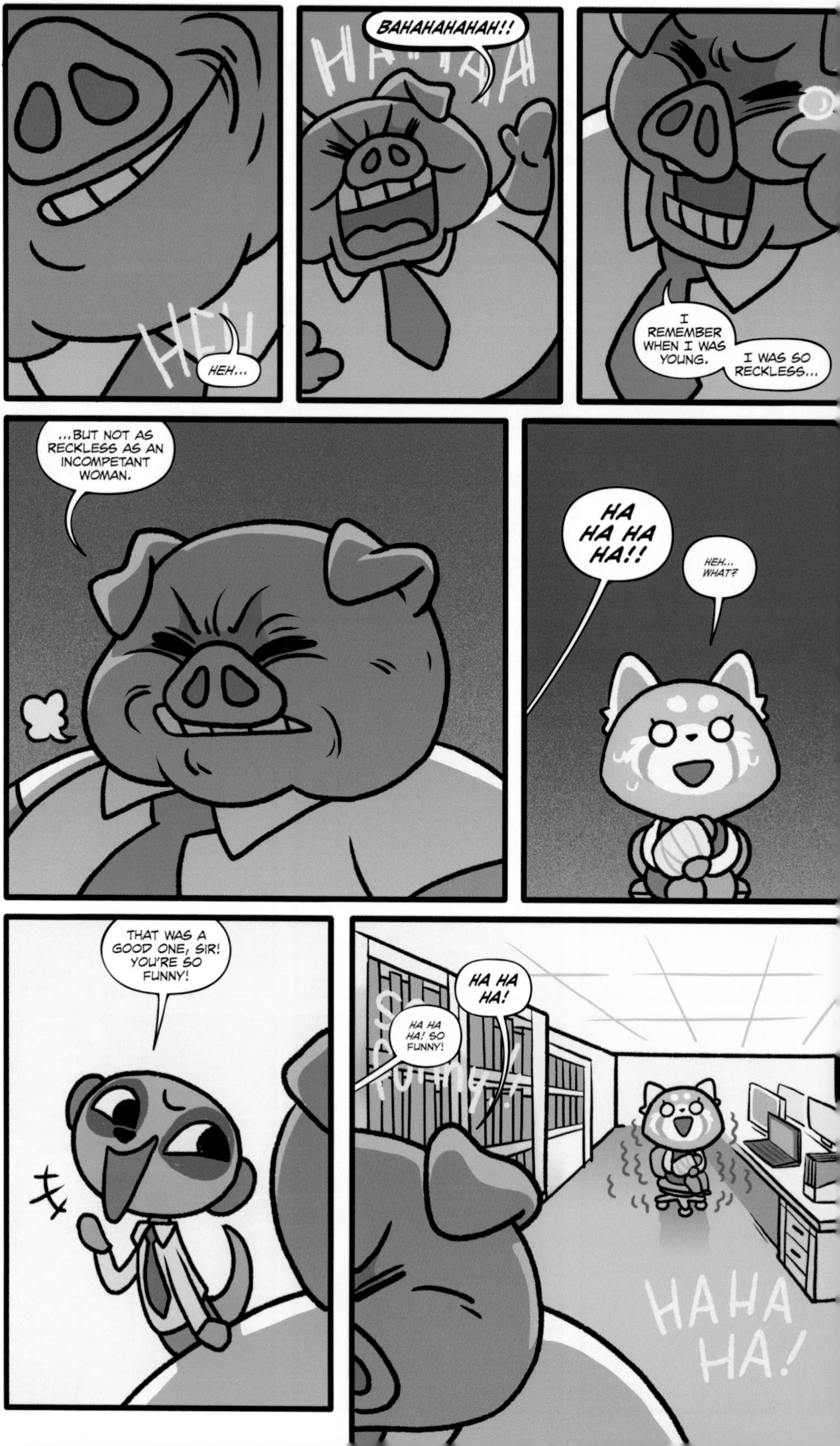
HEH...
BAHAHAHAHAH!!
HA-HA
I REMEMBER WHEN I WAS YOUNG.
I WAS SO RECKLESS...
...BUT NOT AS RECKLESS AS AN INCOMPETANT WOMAN.
HA HA HA HA!!
HEH... WHAT?
THAT WAS A GOOD ONE, SIR! YOU'RE SO FUNNY!
HA HA HA!
HA HA HA! SO FUNNY!
HA HA HA!

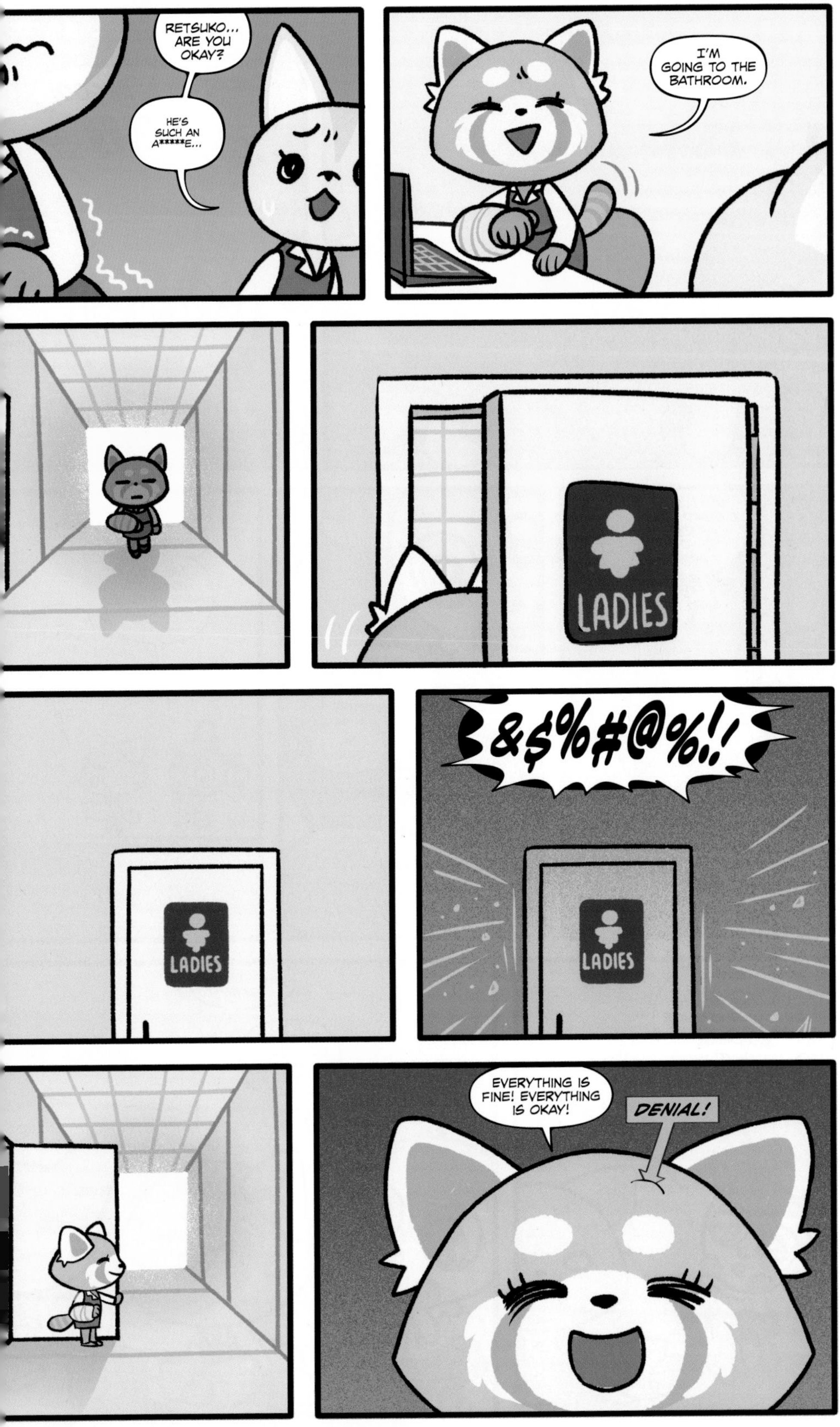
RETSUKO... ARE YOU OKAY?
HE'S SUCH AN A*****E...
I'M GOING TO THE BATHROOM.
LADIES
LADIES
&$%#@%!!
LADIES
EVERYTHING IS FINE! EVERYTHING IS OKAY!
DENIAL!

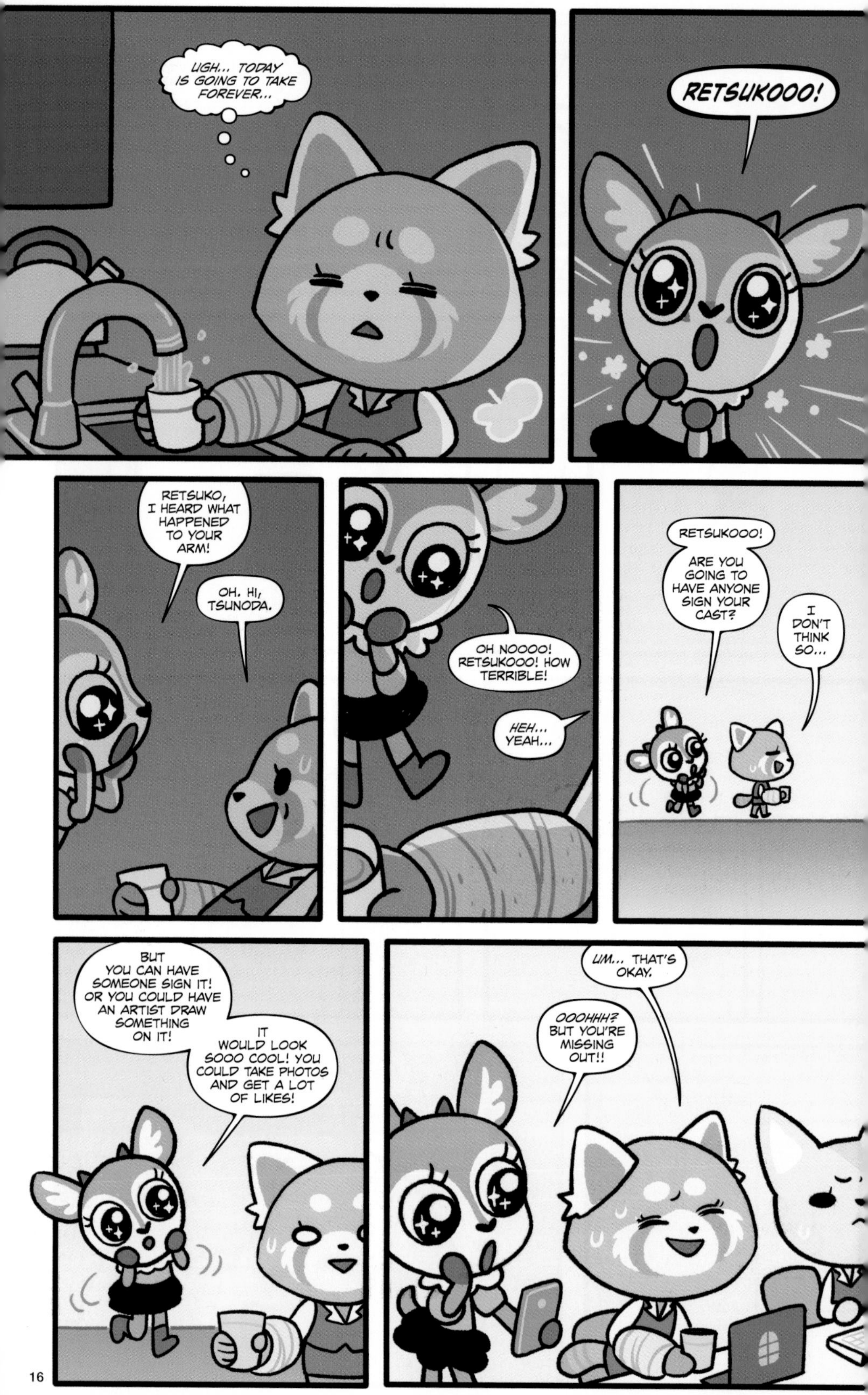
UGH... TODAY IS GOING TO TAKE FOREVER...
RETSUKOOO!
RETSUKO, I HEARD WHAT HAPPENED TO YOUR ARM!
OH. HI, TSUNODA.
OH NOOOO! RETSUKOOO! HOW TERRIBLE!
HEH... YEAH...
RETSUKOOO!
ARE YOU GOING TO HAVE ANYONE SIGN YOUR CAST?
I DON'T THINK SO...
BUT YOU CAN HAVE SOMEONE SIGN IT! OR YOU COULD HAVE AN ARTIST DRAW SOMETHING ON IT!
IT WOULD LOOK SOOO COOL! YOU COULD TAKE PHOTOS AND GET A LOT OF LIKES!
UM... THAT'S OKAY.
OOOHHH? BUT YOU'RE MISSING OUT!!

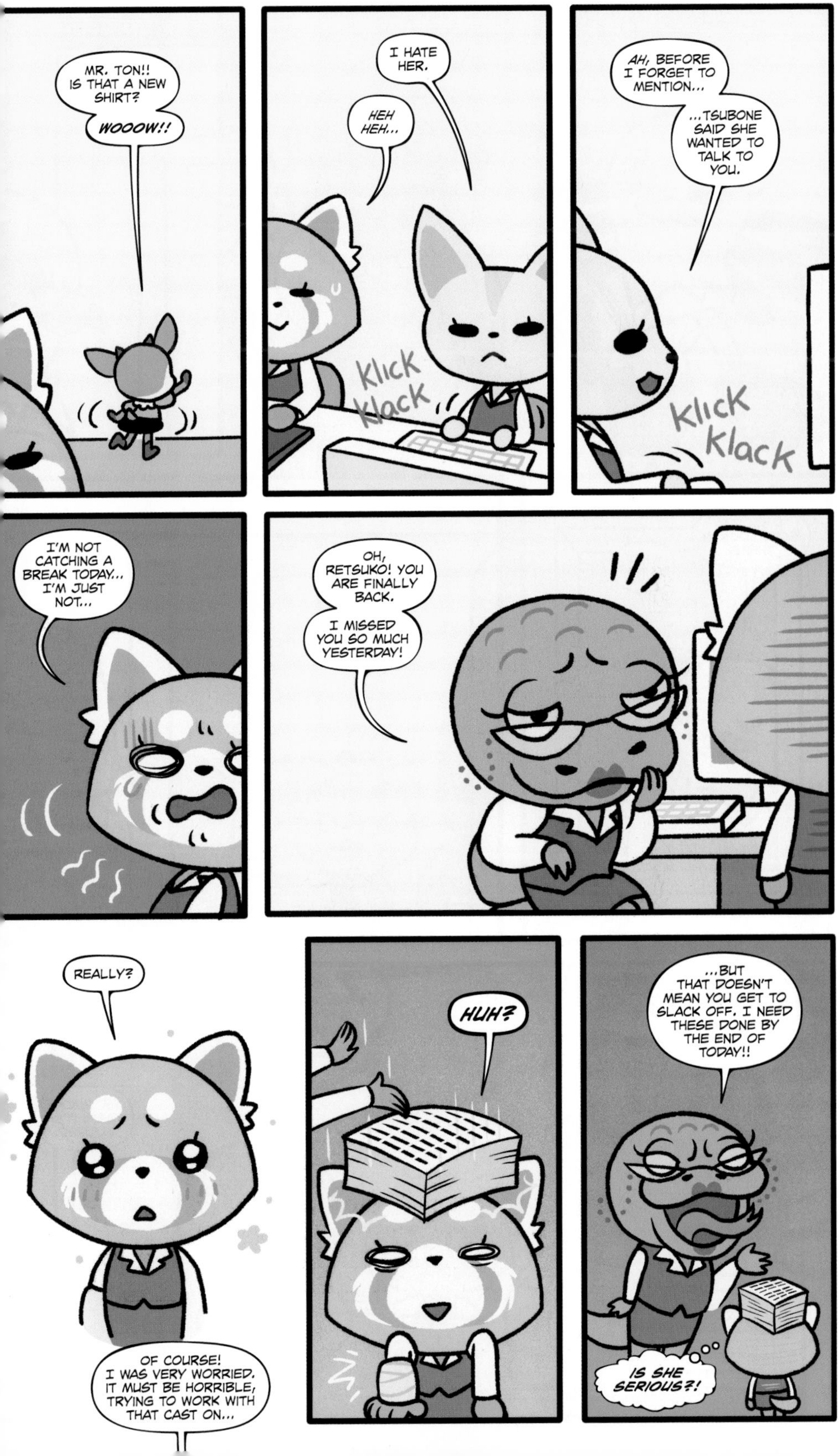
MR. TON!! IS THAT A NEW SHIRT?
WOOOW!!
HEH HEH...
I HATE HER.
Klick Klack
AH, BEFORE I FORGET TO MENTION...
...TSUBONE SAID SHE WANTED TO TALK TO YOU.
Klick Klack
I'M NOT CATCHING A BREAK TODAY... I'M JUST NOT...
OH, RETSUKO! YOU ARE FINALLY BACK.
I MISSED YOU SO MUCH YESTERDAY!
REALLY?
OF COURSE! I WAS VERY WORRIED. IT MUST BE HORRIBLE, TRYING TO WORK WITH THAT CAST ON...
HUH?
...BUT THAT DOESN'T MEAN YOU GET TO SLACK OFF. I NEED THESE DONE BY THE END OF TODAY!!
IS SHE SERIOUS?!

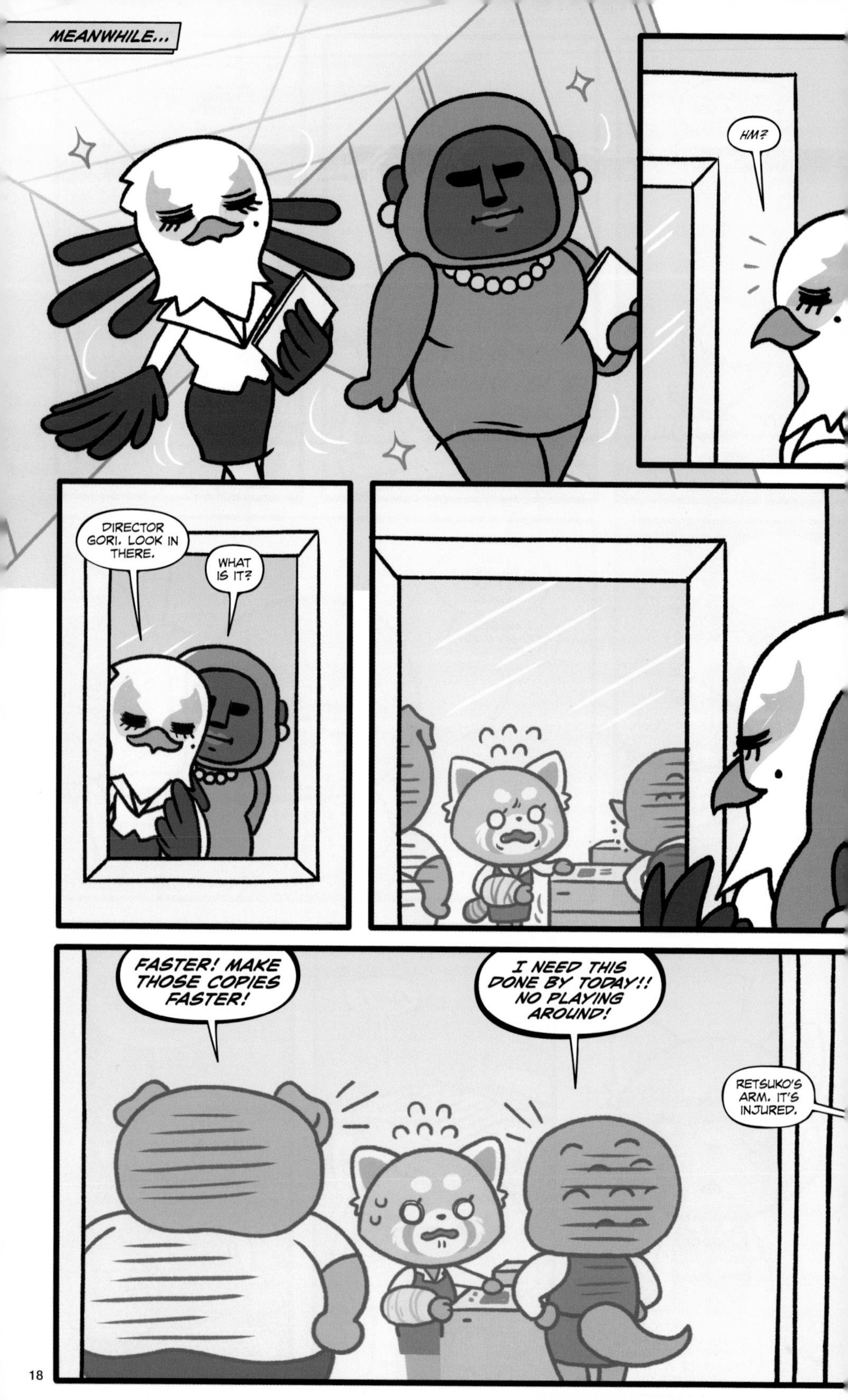
MEANWHILE...
HM?
DIRECTOR GORI. LOOK IN THERE.
WHAT IS IT?
FASTER! MAKE THOSE COPIES FASTER!
I NEED THIS DONE BY TODAY!! NO PLAYING AROUND!
RETSUKO'S ARM. IT'S INJURED.

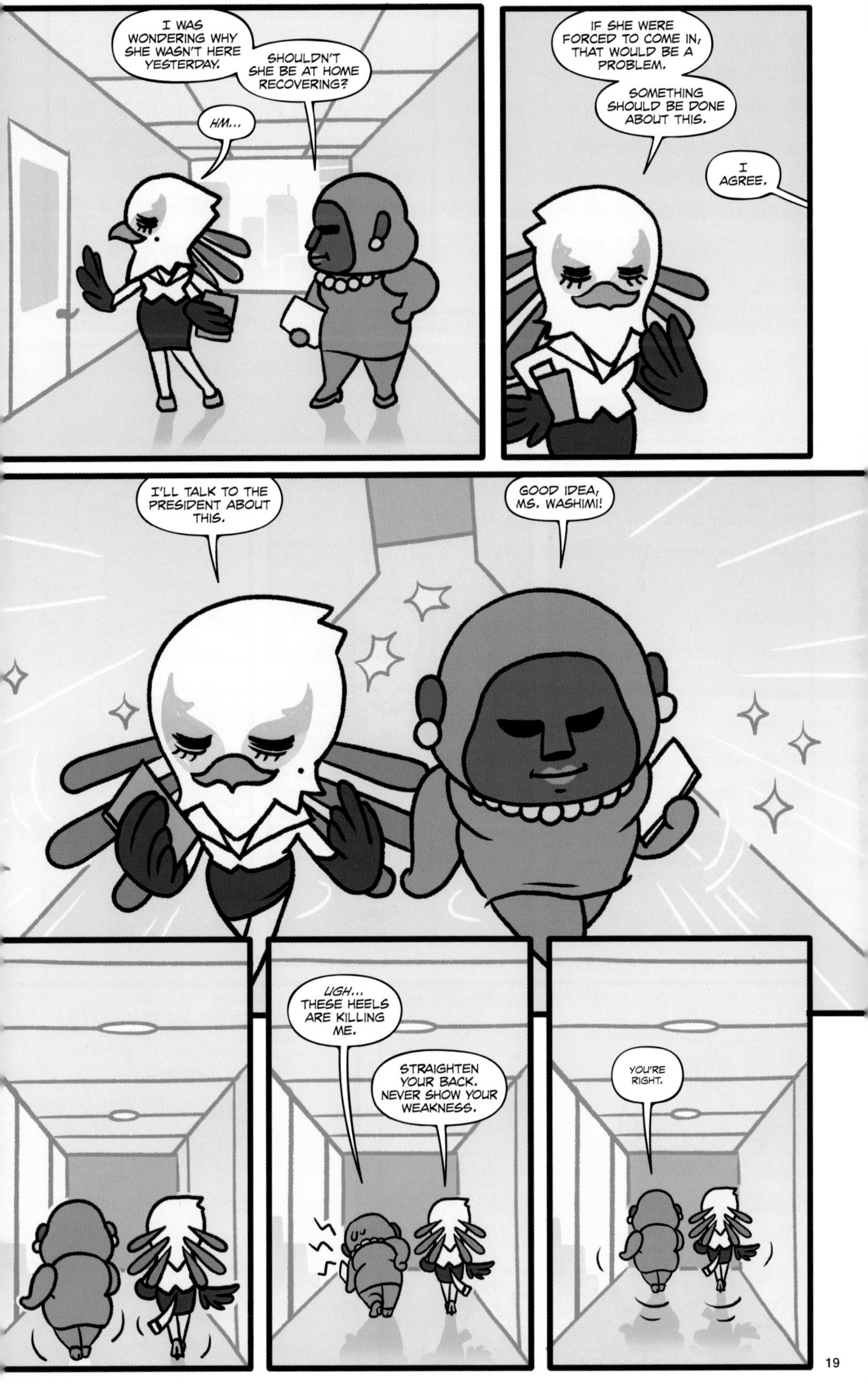
I WAS WONDERING WHY SHE WASN'T HERE YESTERDAY.
SHOULDN'T SHE BE AT HOME RECOVERING?
HM...
IF SHE WERE FORCED TO COME IN, THAT WOULD BE A PROBLEM.
SOMETHING SHOULD BE DONE ABOUT THIS.
I AGREE.
I'LL TALK TO THE PRESIDENT ABOUT THIS.
GOOD IDEA, MS. WASHIMI!
UGH... THESE HEELS ARE KILLING ME.
STRAIGHTEN YOUR BACK. NEVER SHOW YOUR WEAKNESS.
YOU'RE RIGHT.

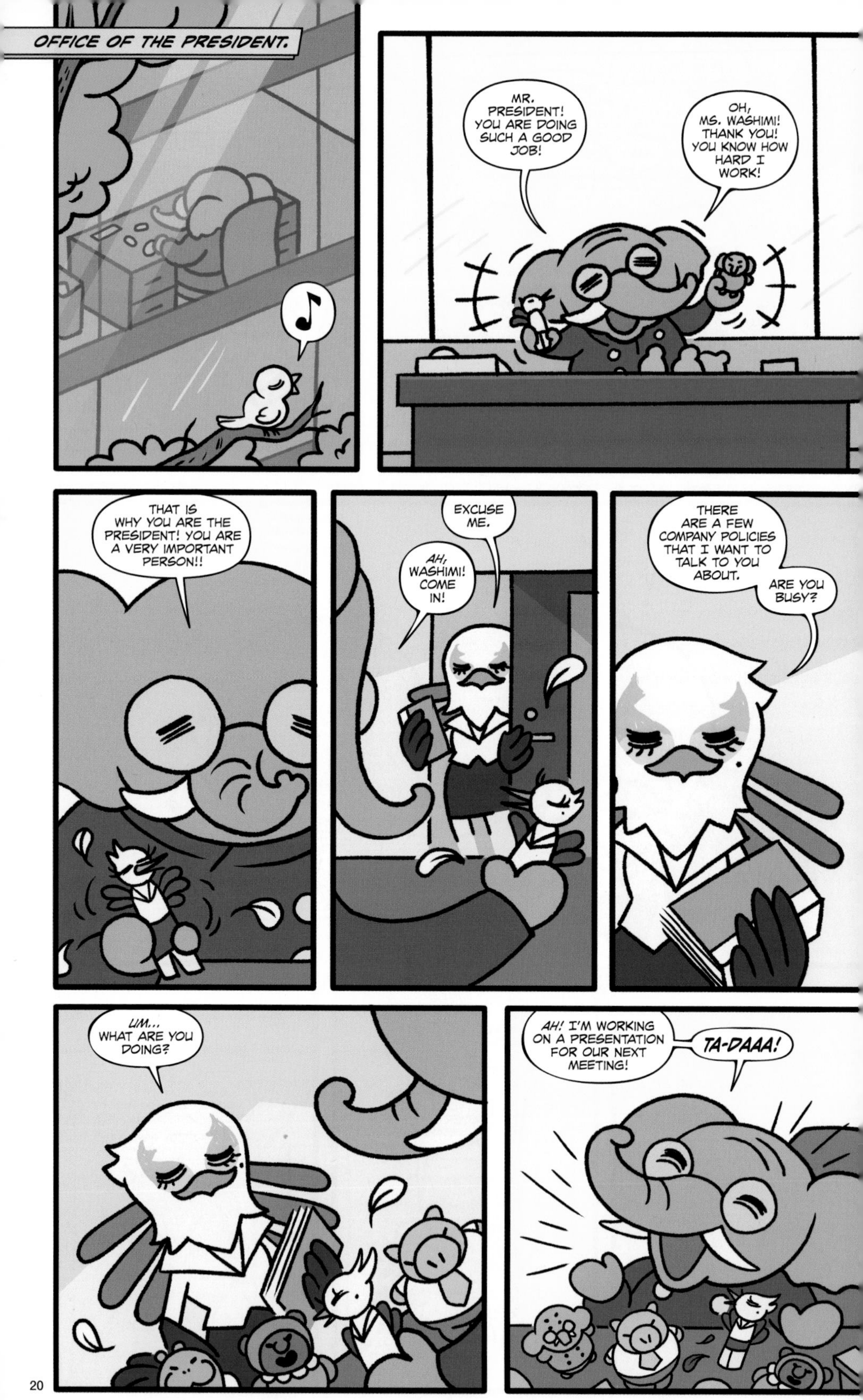
OFFICE OF THE PRESIDENT.
♪
MR. PRESIDENT! YOU ARE DOING SUCH A GOOD JOB!
OH, MS. WASHIMI! THANK YOU! YOU KNOW HOW HARD I WORK!
THAT IS WHY YOU ARE THE PRESIDENT! YOU ARE A VERY IMPORTANT PERSON!!
EXCUSE ME.
AH, WASHIMI! COME IN!
THERE ARE A FEW COMPANY POLICIES THAT I WANT TO TALK TO YOU ABOUT.
ARE YOU BUSY?
UM... WHAT ARE YOU DOING?
AH! I'M WORKING ON A PRESENTATION FOR OUR NEXT MEETING!
TA-DAAA!

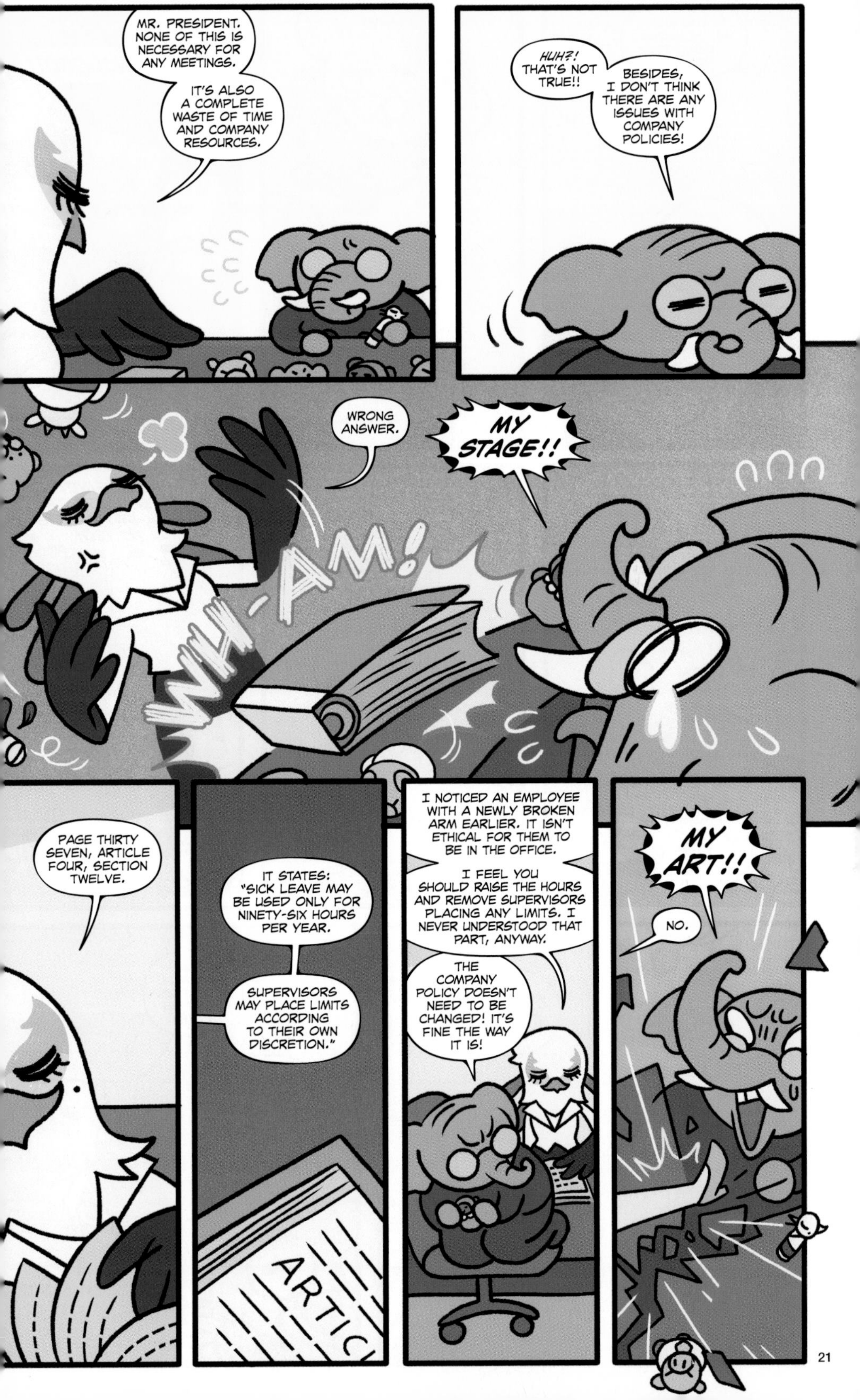
MR. PRESIDENT. NONE OF THIS IS NECESSARY FOR ANY MEETINGS.
IT'S ALSO A COMPLETE WASTE OF TIME AND COMPANY RESOURCES.
HUH?! THAT'S NOT TRUE!!
BESIDES, I DON'T THINK THERE ARE ANY ISSUES WITH COMPANY POLICIES!
WRONG ANSWER.
MY STAGE!!
WHAM!
PAGE THIRTY SEVEN, ARTICLE FOUR, SECTION TWELVE.
IT STATES: "SICK LEAVE MAY BE USED ONLY FOR NINETY-SIX HOURS PER YEAR.
SUPERVISORS MAY PLACE LIMITS ACCORDING TO THEIR OWN DISCRETION."
ARTIC
I NOTICED AN EMPLOYEE WITH A NEWLY BROKEN ARM EARLIER. IT ISN'T ETHICAL FOR THEM TO BE IN THE OFFICE.
I FEEL YOU SHOULD RAISE THE HOURS AND REMOVE SUPERVISORS PLACING ANY LIMITS. I NEVER UNDERSTOOD THAT PART, ANYWAY.
THE COMPANY POLICY DOESN'T NEED TO BE CHANGED! IT'S FINE THE WAY IT IS!
MY ART!!
NO.

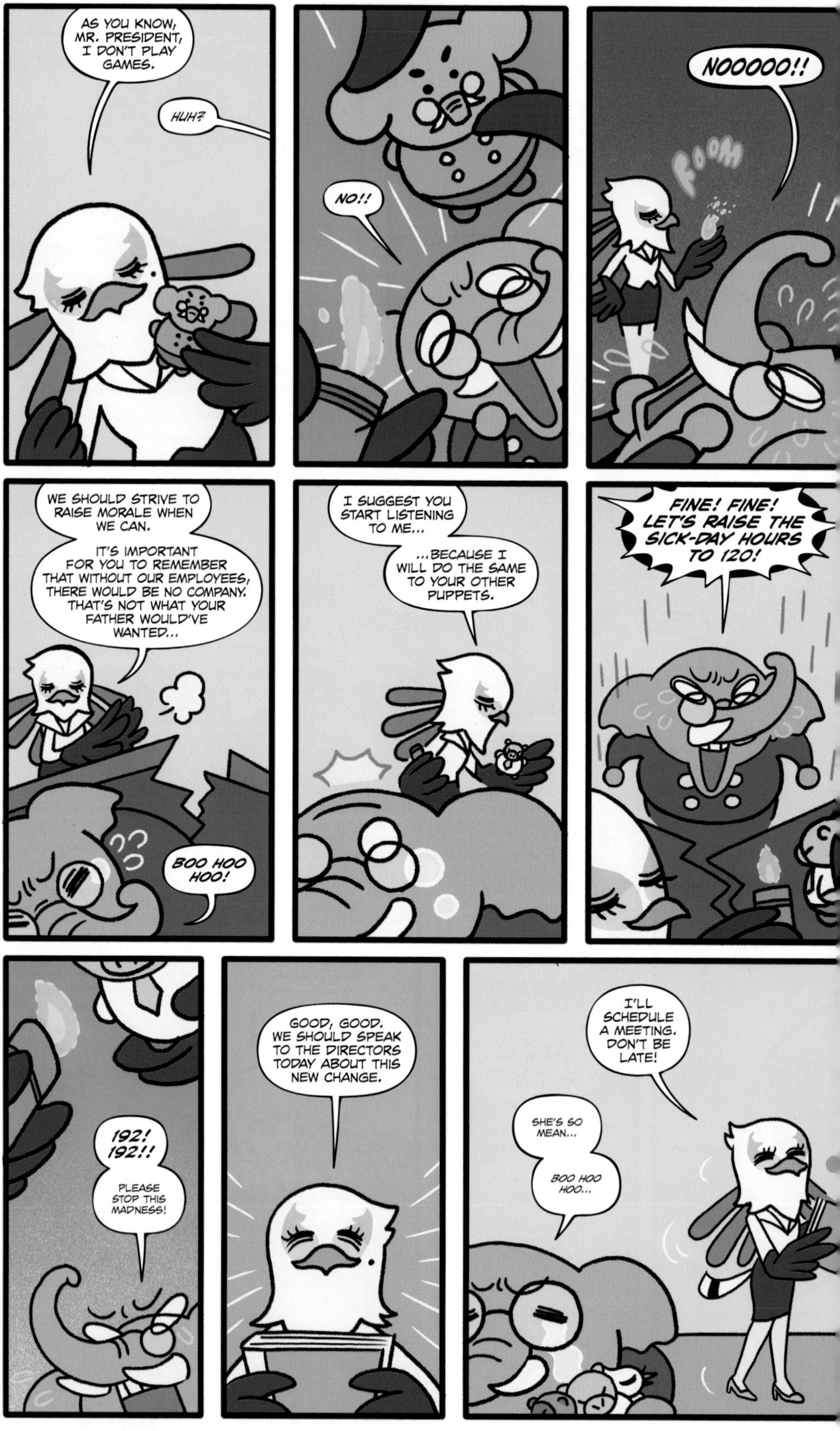
AS YOU KNOW, MR. PRESIDENT, I DON'T PLAY GAMES.
HUH?
NO!!
NOOOOO!!
FOOM
WE SHOULD STRIVE TO RAISE MORALE WHEN WE CAN.
IT'S IMPORTANT FOR YOU TO REMEMBER THAT WITHOUT OUR EMPLOYEES, THERE WOULD BE NO COMPANY. THAT'S NOT WHAT YOUR FATHER WOULD'VE WANTED...
BOO HOO HOO!
I SUGGEST YOU START LISTENING TO ME...
...BECAUSE I WILL DO THE SAME TO YOUR OTHER PUPPETS.
FINE! FINE! LET'S RAISE THE SICK-DAY HOURS TO 120!
192! 192!!
PLEASE STOP THIS MADNESS!
GOOD, GOOD. WE SHOULD SPEAK TO THE DIRECTORS TODAY ABOUT THIS NEW CHANGE.
I'LL SCHEDULE A MEETING. DON'T BE LATE!
SHE'S SO MEAN...
BOO HOO HOO...

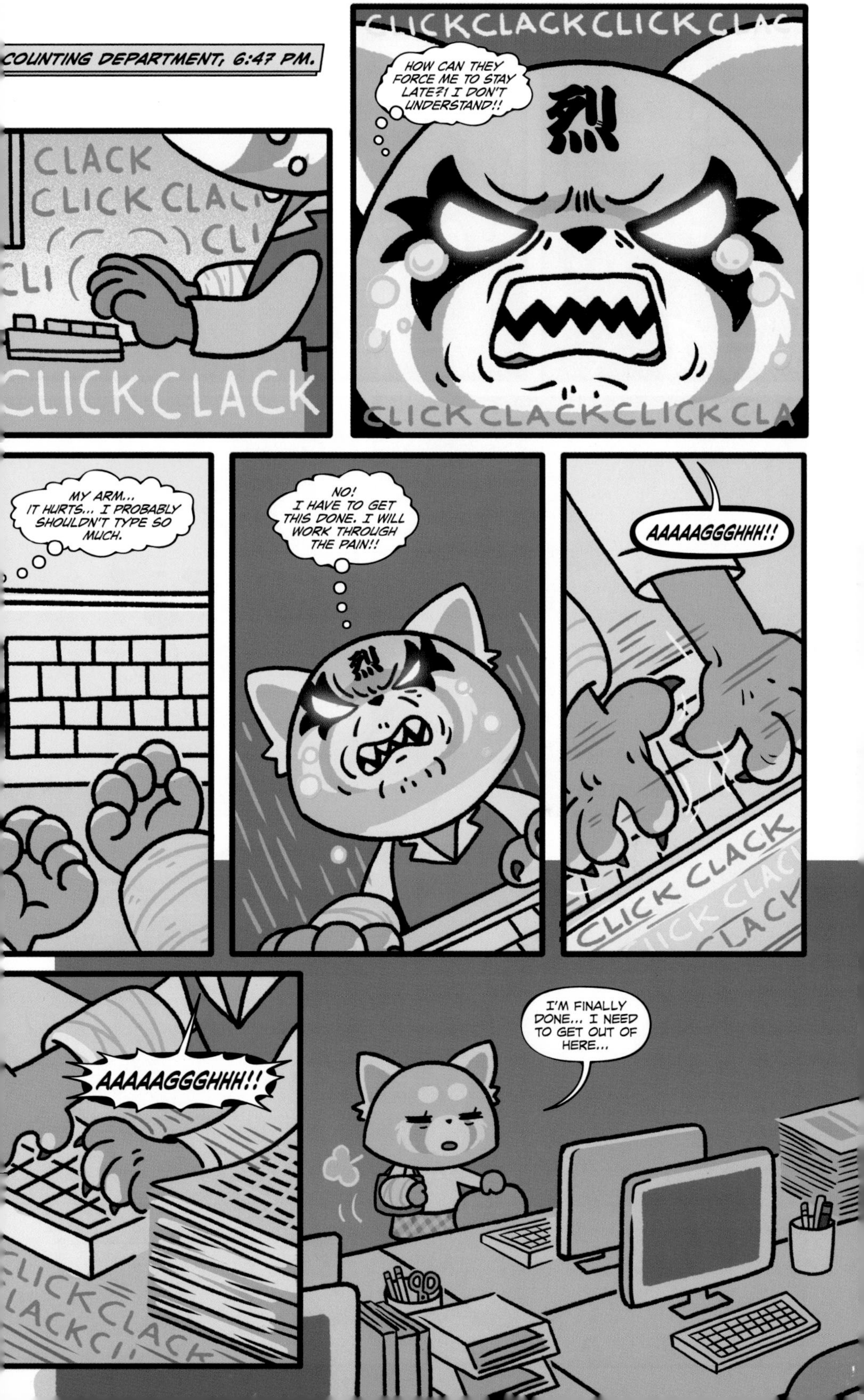
COUNTING DEPARTMENT, 6:47 PM.
CLACK CLICK CLACK
CLICKCLACK
CLICKCLACKCLICK
HOW CAN THEY FORCE ME TO STAY LATE?! I DON'T UNDERSTAND!!
CLICK CLACKCLICK
MY ARM... IT HURTS... I PROBABLY SHOULDN'T TYPE SO MUCH.
NO! I HAVE TO GET THIS DONE. I WILL WORK THROUGH THE PAIN!!
AAAAAGGGHHH!!
CLICK CLACK
AAAAAGGGHHH!!
CLICK CLACK
I'M FINALLY DONE... I NEED TO GET OUT OF HERE...

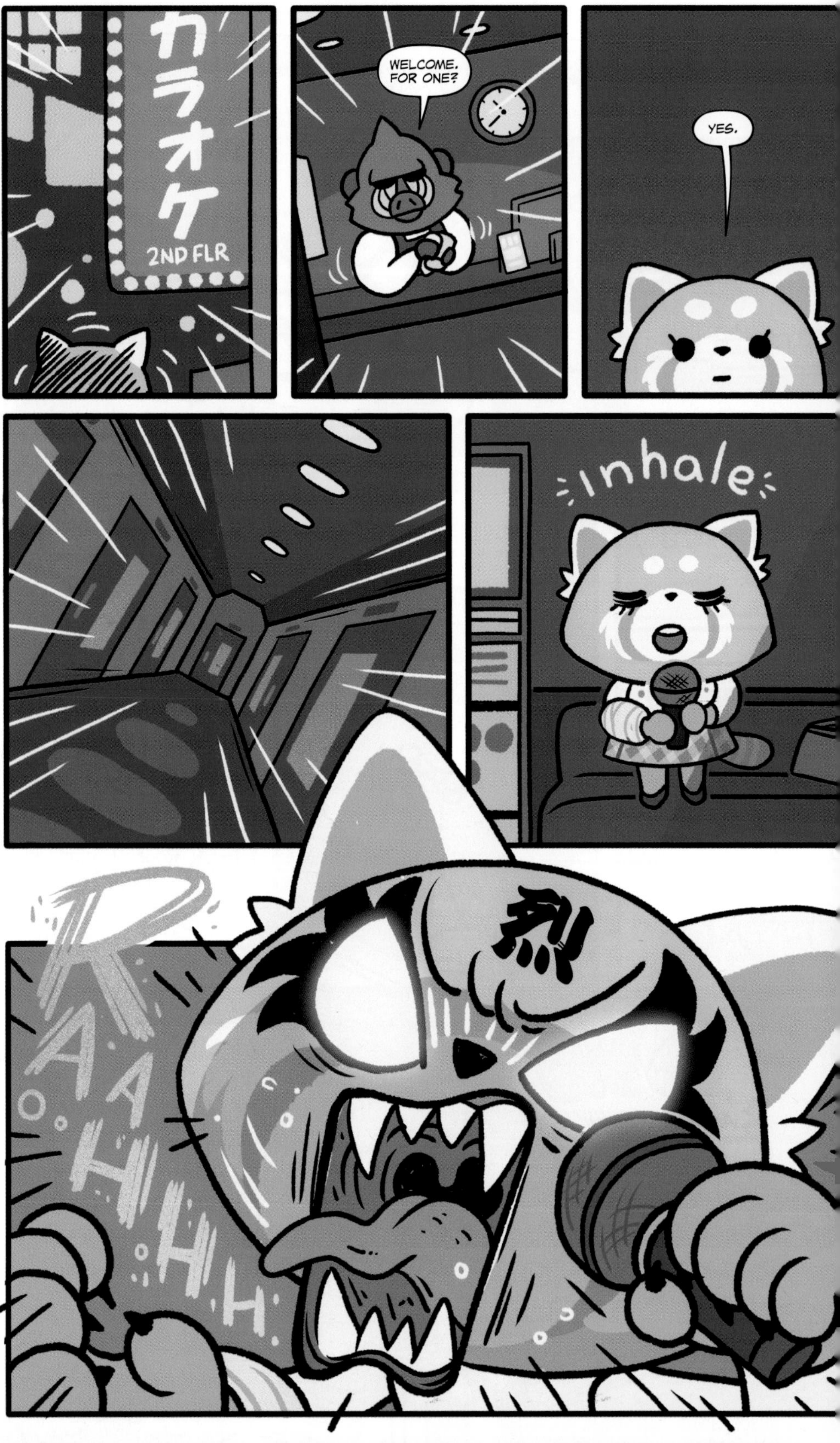
カラオケ
2ND FLR
WELCOME. FOR ONE?
YES.
inhale
RAAHHHHHH

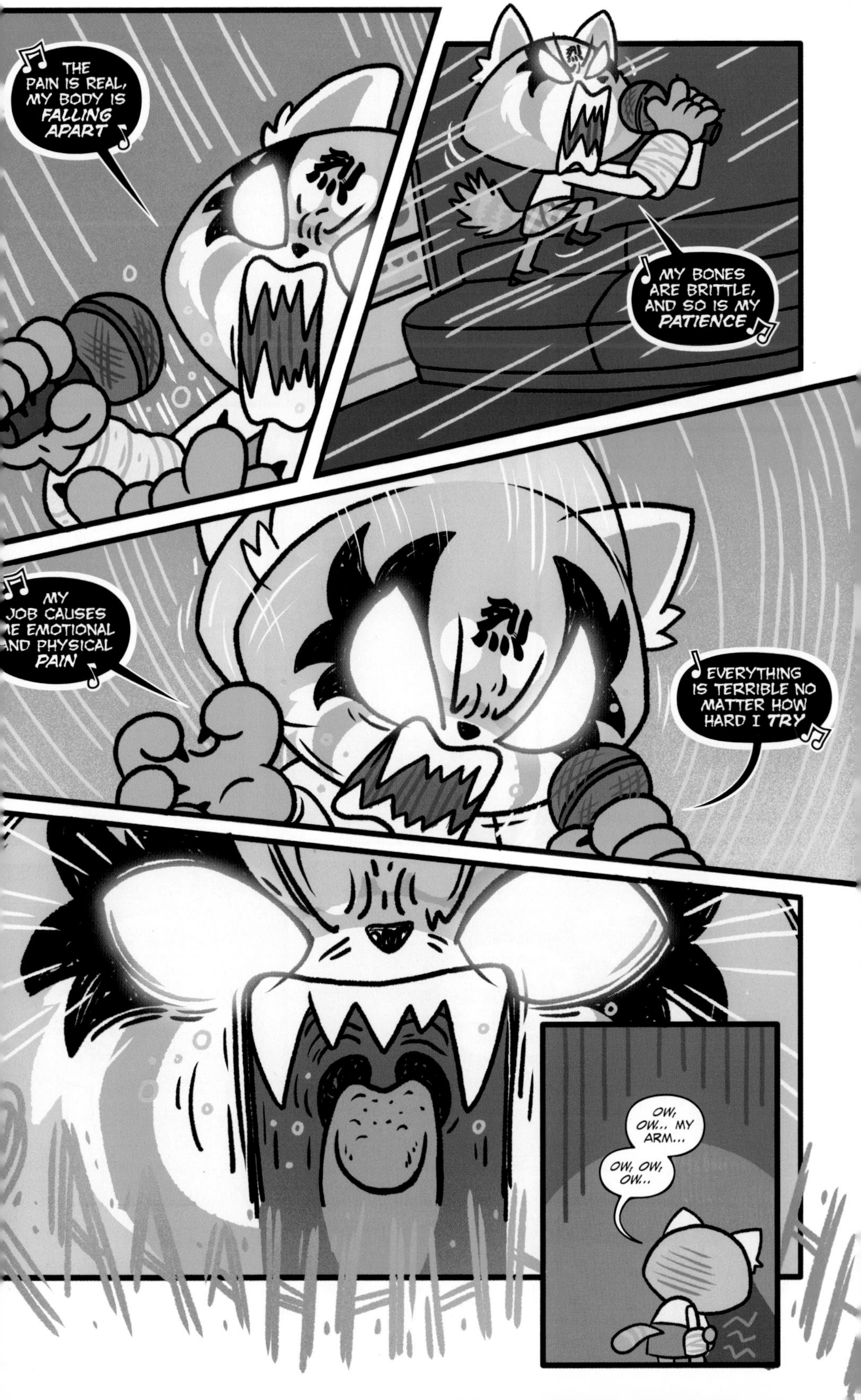
THE PAIN IS REAL, MY BODY IS FALLING APART
MY BONES ARE BRITTLE, AND SO IS MY PATIENCE
MY JOB CAUSES ME EMOTIONAL AND PHYSICAL PAIN
EVERYTHING IS TERRIBLE NO MATTER HOW HARD I TRY
OW, OW... MY ARM...
OW, OW, OW...

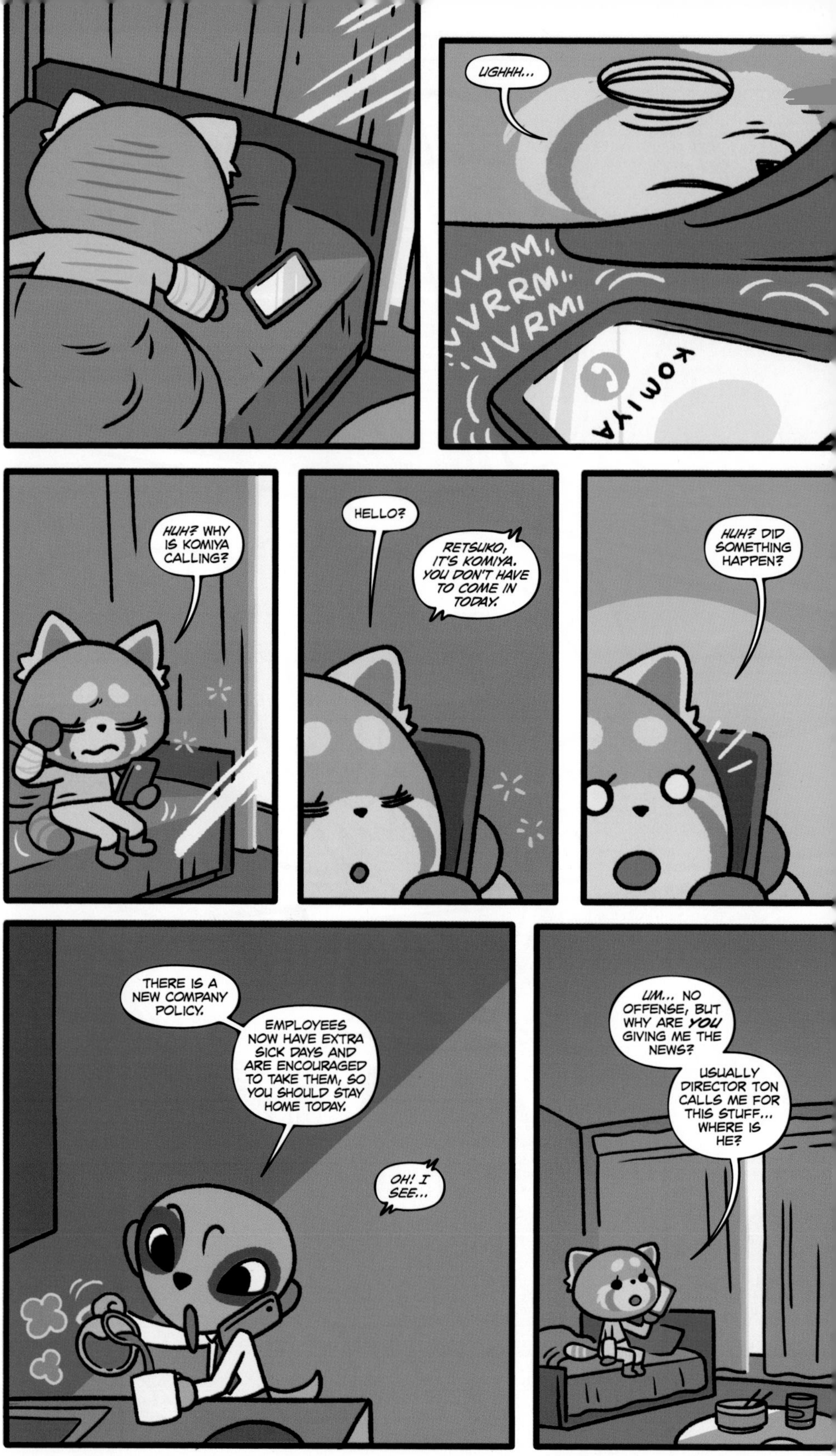
UGHHH...
VVRM! VVRRM! VVRM!
KOMIYA
HUH? WHY IS KOMIYA CALLING?
HELLO?
RETSUKO, IT'S KOMIYA. YOU DON'T HAVE TO COME IN TODAY.
HUH? DID SOMETHING HAPPEN?
THERE IS A NEW COMPANY POLICY.
EMPLOYEES NOW HAVE EXTRA SICK DAYS AND ARE ENCOURAGED TO TAKE THEM, SO YOU SHOULD STAY HOME TODAY.
OH! I SEE...
UM... NO OFFENSE, BUT WHY ARE YOU GIVING ME THE NEWS?
USUALLY DIRECTOR TON CALLS ME FOR THIS STUFF... WHERE IS HE?

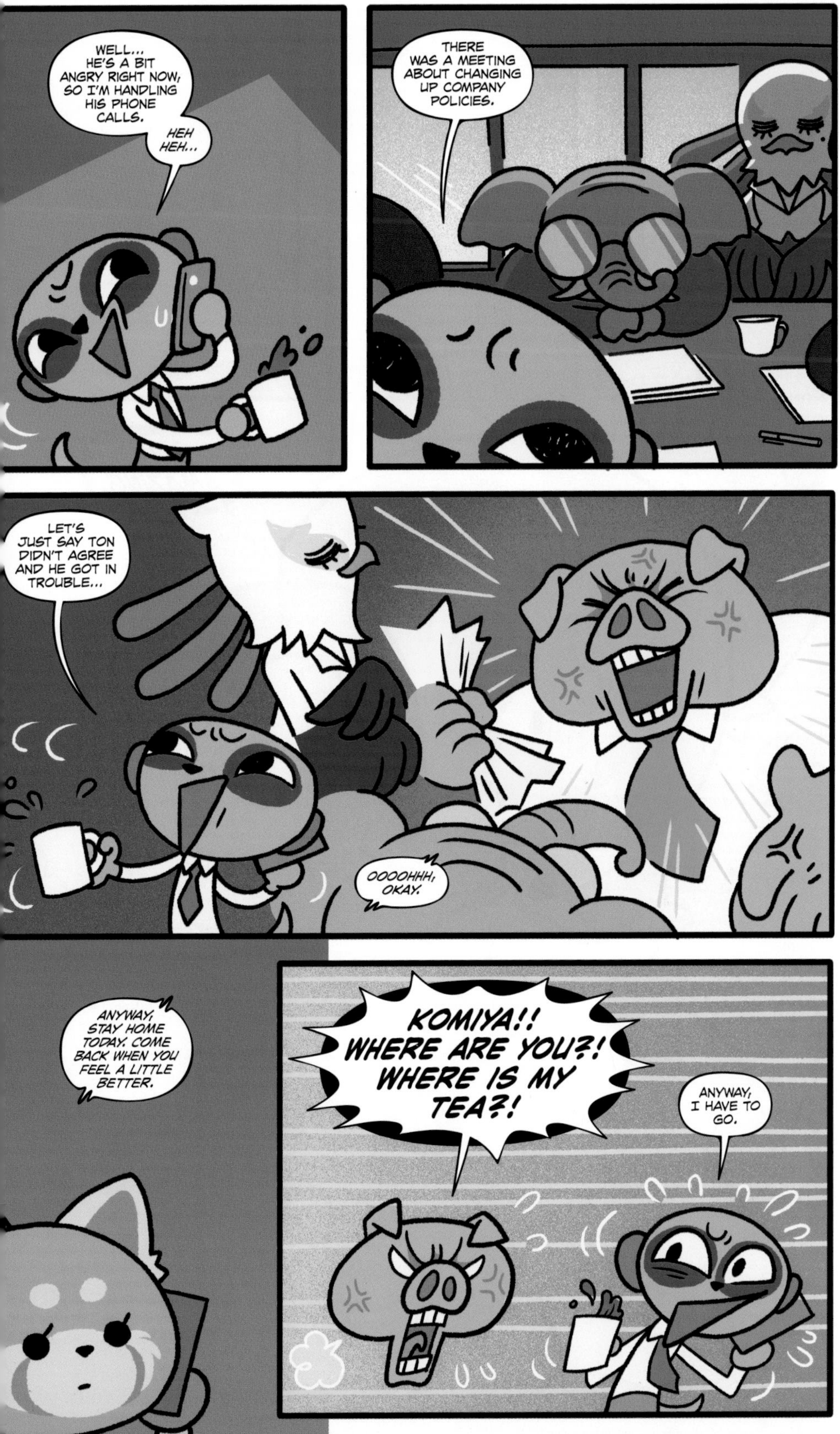
WELL... HE'S A BIT ANGRY RIGHT NOW, SO I'M HANDLING HIS PHONE CALLS.
HEH HEH...
THERE WAS A MEETING ABOUT CHANGING UP COMPANY POLICIES.
LET'S JUST SAY TON DIDN'T AGREE AND HE GOT IN TROUBLE...
OOOOHHH, OKAY.
ANYWAY, STAY HOME TODAY. COME BACK WHEN YOU FEEL A LITTLE BETTER.
KOMIYA!! WHERE ARE YOU?! WHERE IS MY TEA?!
ANYWAY, I HAVE TO GO.

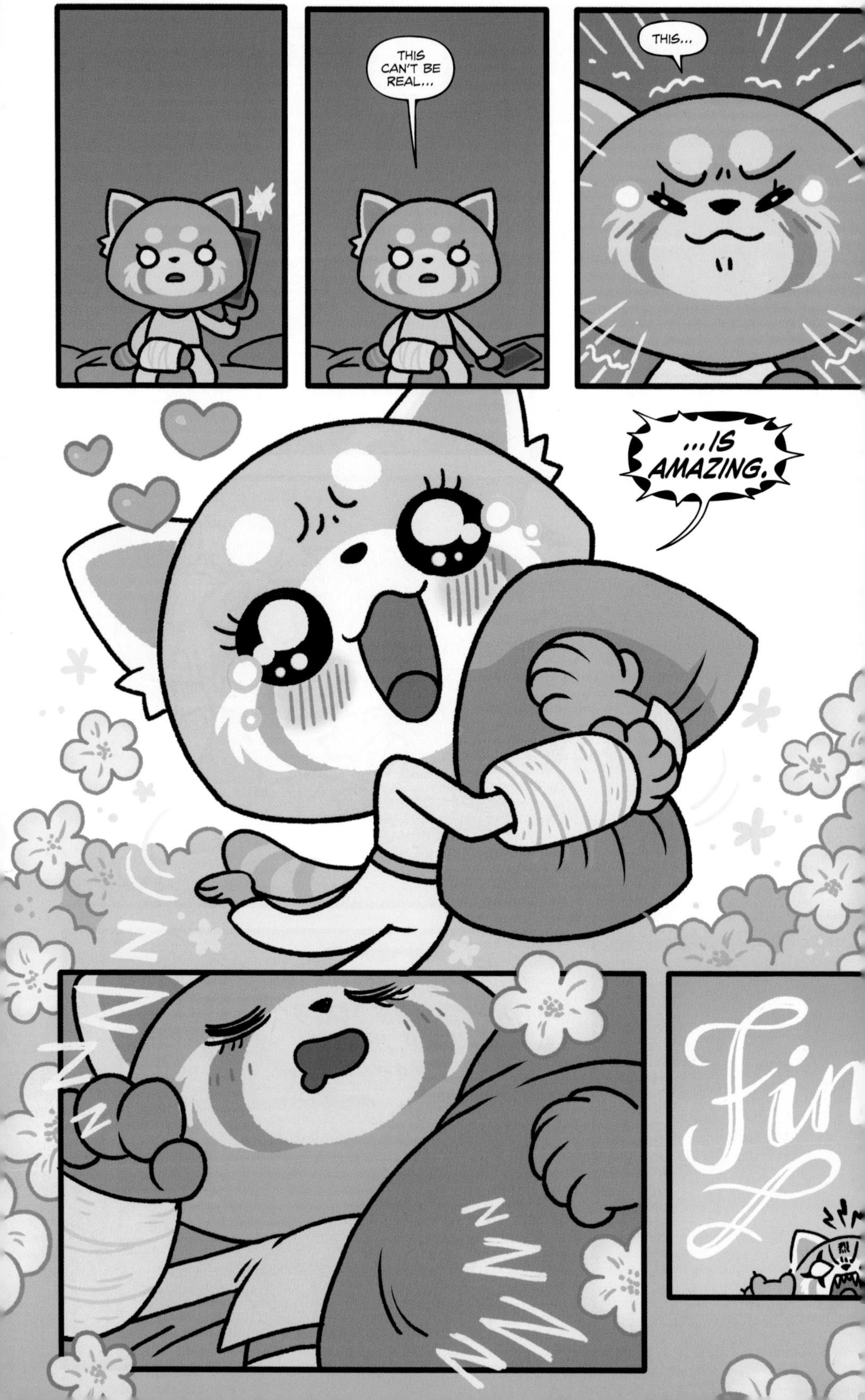
THIS CAN'T BE REAL...
THIS...
...IS AMAZING.
Fin

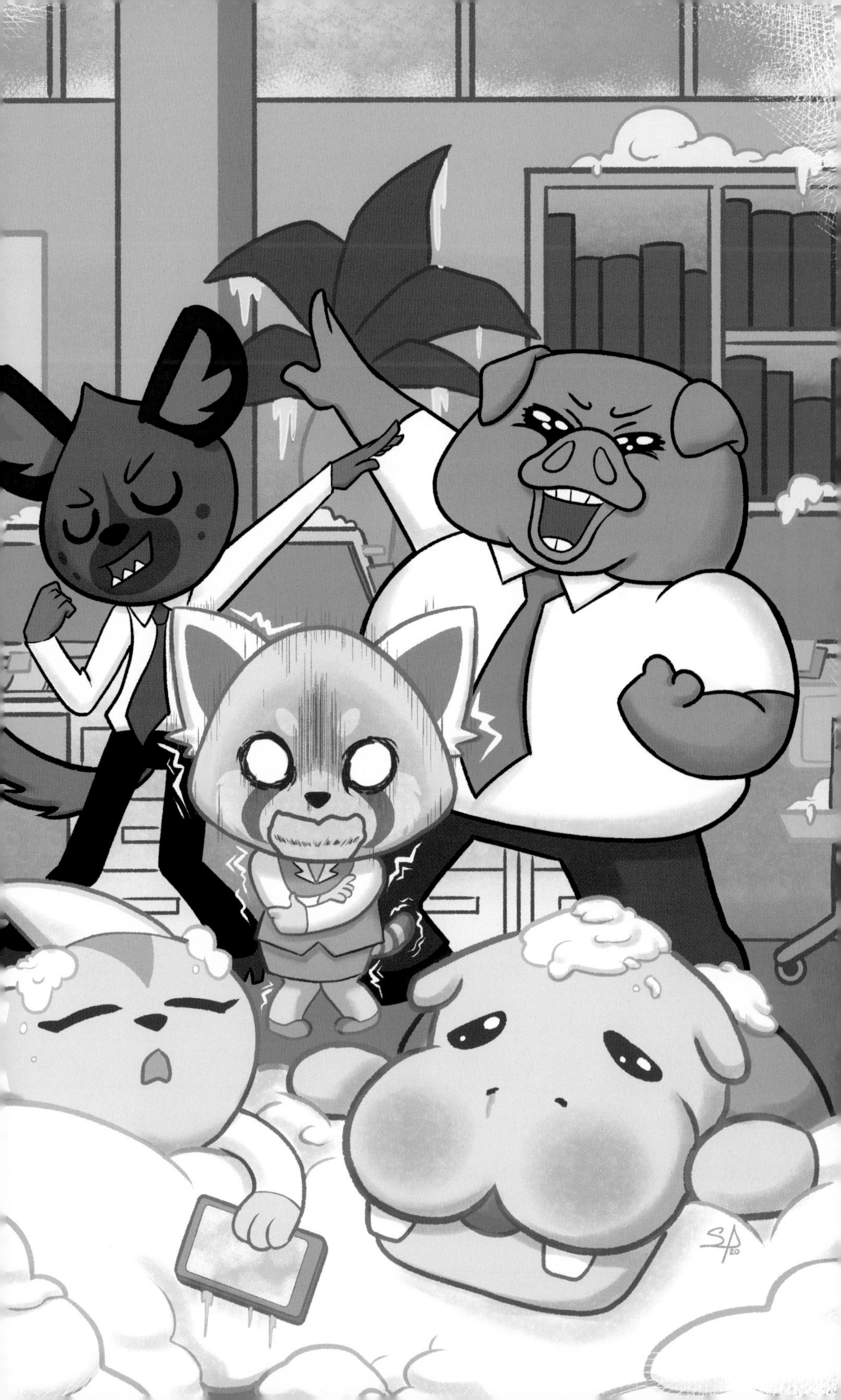

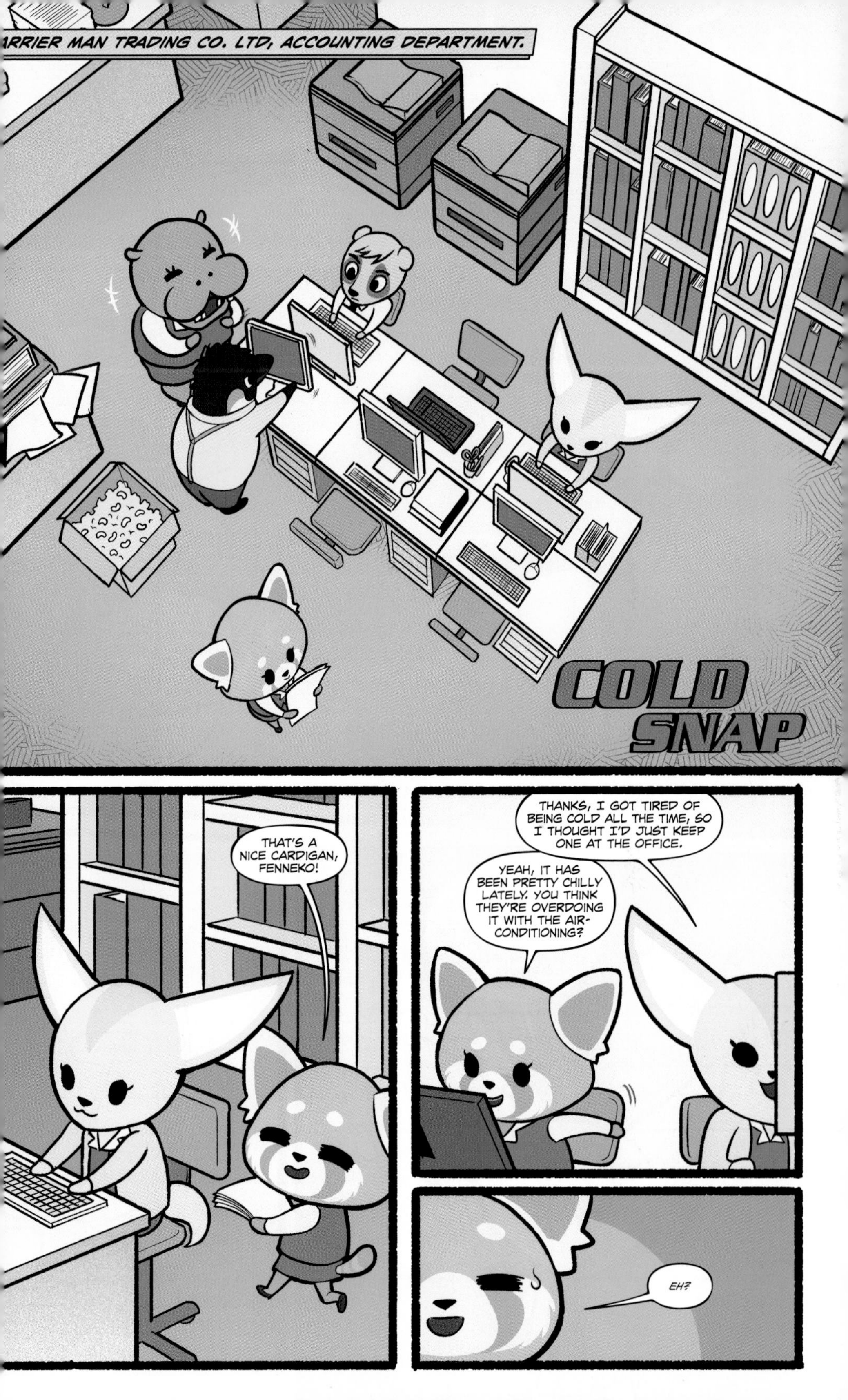
ARRIER MAN TRADING CO. LTD, ACCOUNTING DEPARTMENT.
COLD SNAP
THAT'S A NICE CARDIGAN, FENNEKO!
THANKS, I GOT TIRED OF BEING COLD ALL THE TIME, SO I THOUGHT I'D JUST KEEP ONE AT THE OFFICE.
YEAH, IT HAS BEEN PRETTY CHILLY LATELY. YOU THINK THEY'RE OVERDOING IT WITH THE AIR-CONDITIONING?
EH?

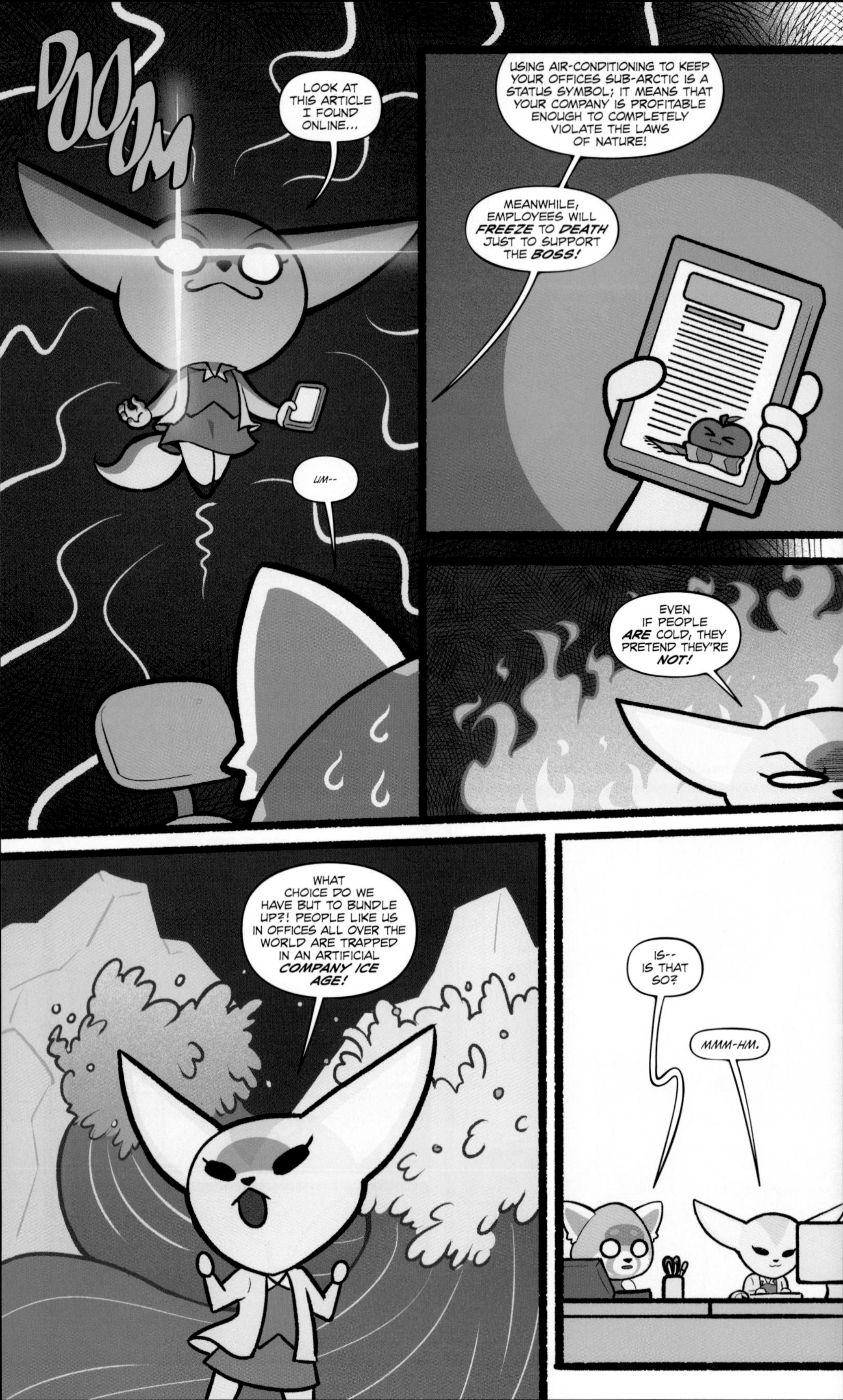
DOOOM
LOOK AT THIS ARTICLE I FOUND ONLINE...
USING AIR-CONDITIONING TO KEEP YOUR OFFICES SUB-ARCTIC IS A STATUS SYMBOL; IT MEANS THAT YOUR COMPANY IS PROFITABLE ENOUGH TO COMPLETELY VIOLATE THE LAWS OF NATURE!
MEANWHILE, EMPLOYEES WILL FREEZE TO DEATH JUST TO SUPPORT THE BOSS!
UM--
EVEN IF PEOPLE ARE COLD, THEY PRETEND THEY'RE NOT!
WHAT CHOICE DO WE HAVE BUT TO BUNDLE UP?! PEOPLE LIKE US IN OFFICES ALL OVER THE WORLD ARE TRAPPED IN AN ARTIFICIAL COMPANY ICE AGE!
IS-- IS THAT SO?
MMM-HM.

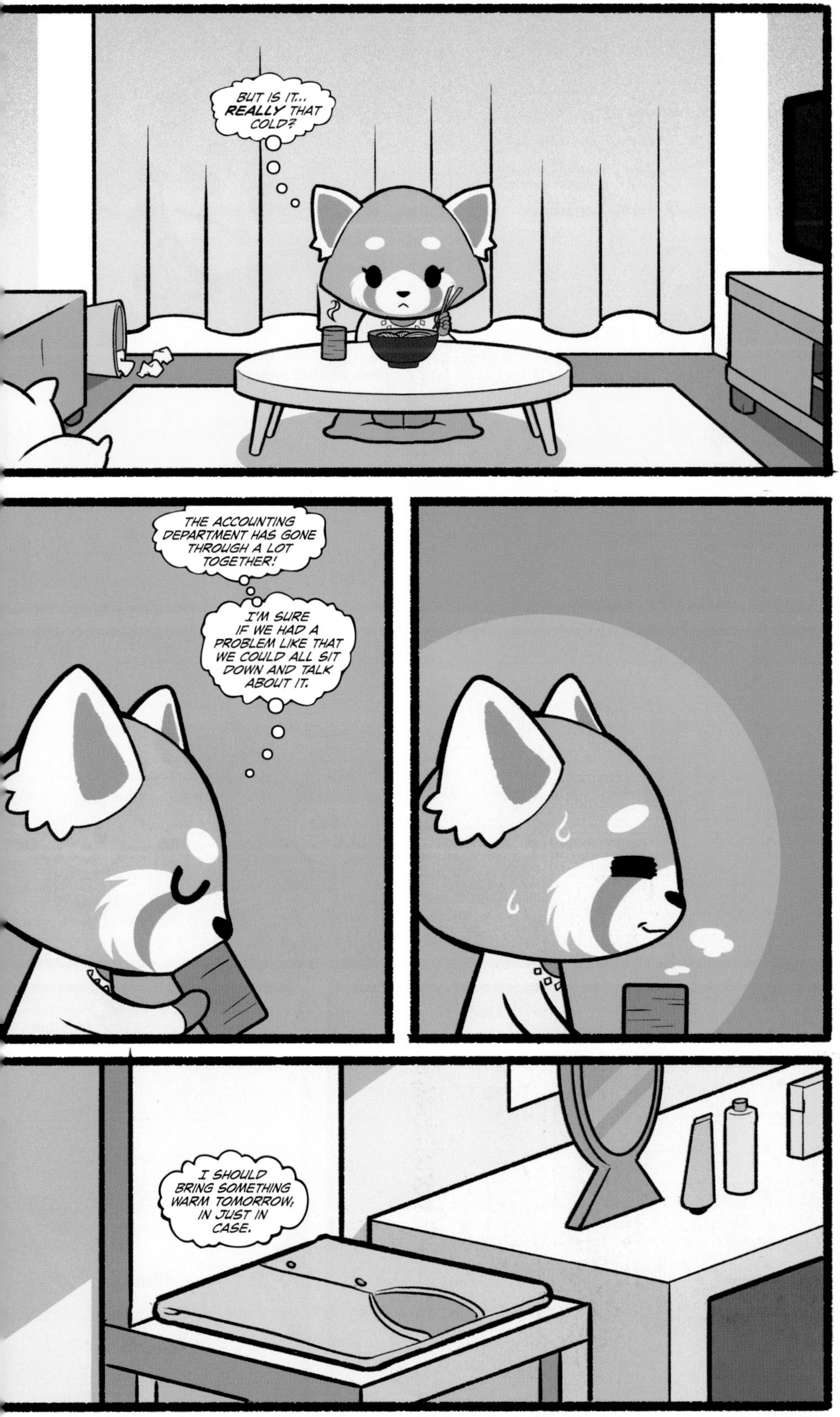
BUT IS IT... REALLY THAT COLD?
THE ACCOUNTING DEPARTMENT HAS GONE THROUGH A LOT TOGETHER!
I'M SURE IF WE HAD A PROBLEM LIKE THAT WE COULD ALL SIT DOWN AND TALK ABOUT IT.
I SHOULD BRING SOMETHING WARM TOMORROW, IN JUST IN CASE.

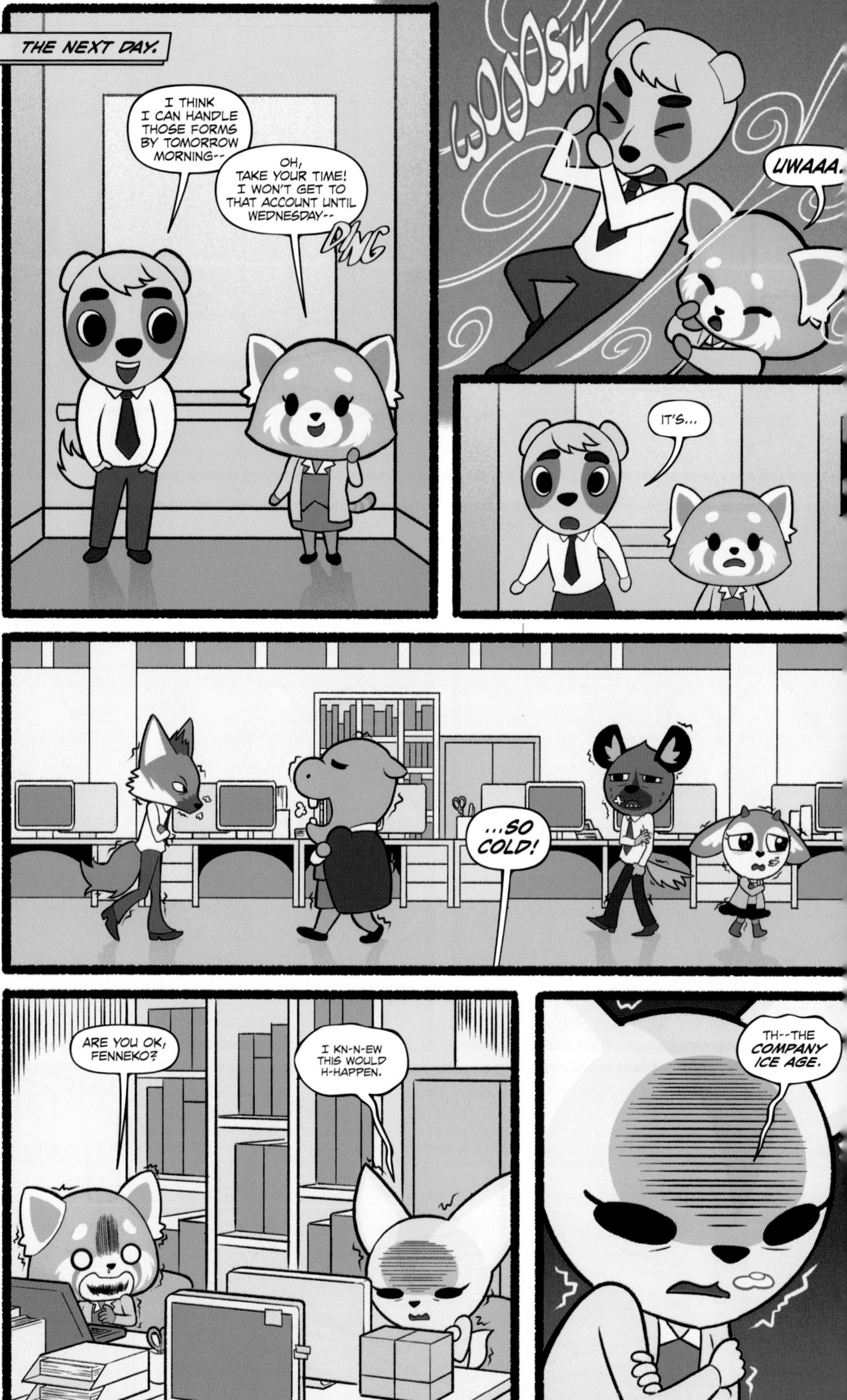
THE NEXT DAY.
I THINK I CAN HANDLE THOSE FORMS BY TOMORROW MORNING--
OH, TAKE YOUR TIME! I WON'T GET TO THAT ACCOUNT UNTIL WEDNESDAY--
DING
WOOOSH
UWAAA.
IT'S...
...SO COLD!
ARE YOU OK, FENNEKO?
I KN-N-EW THIS WOULD H-HAPPEN.
TH--THE COMPANY ICE AGE.

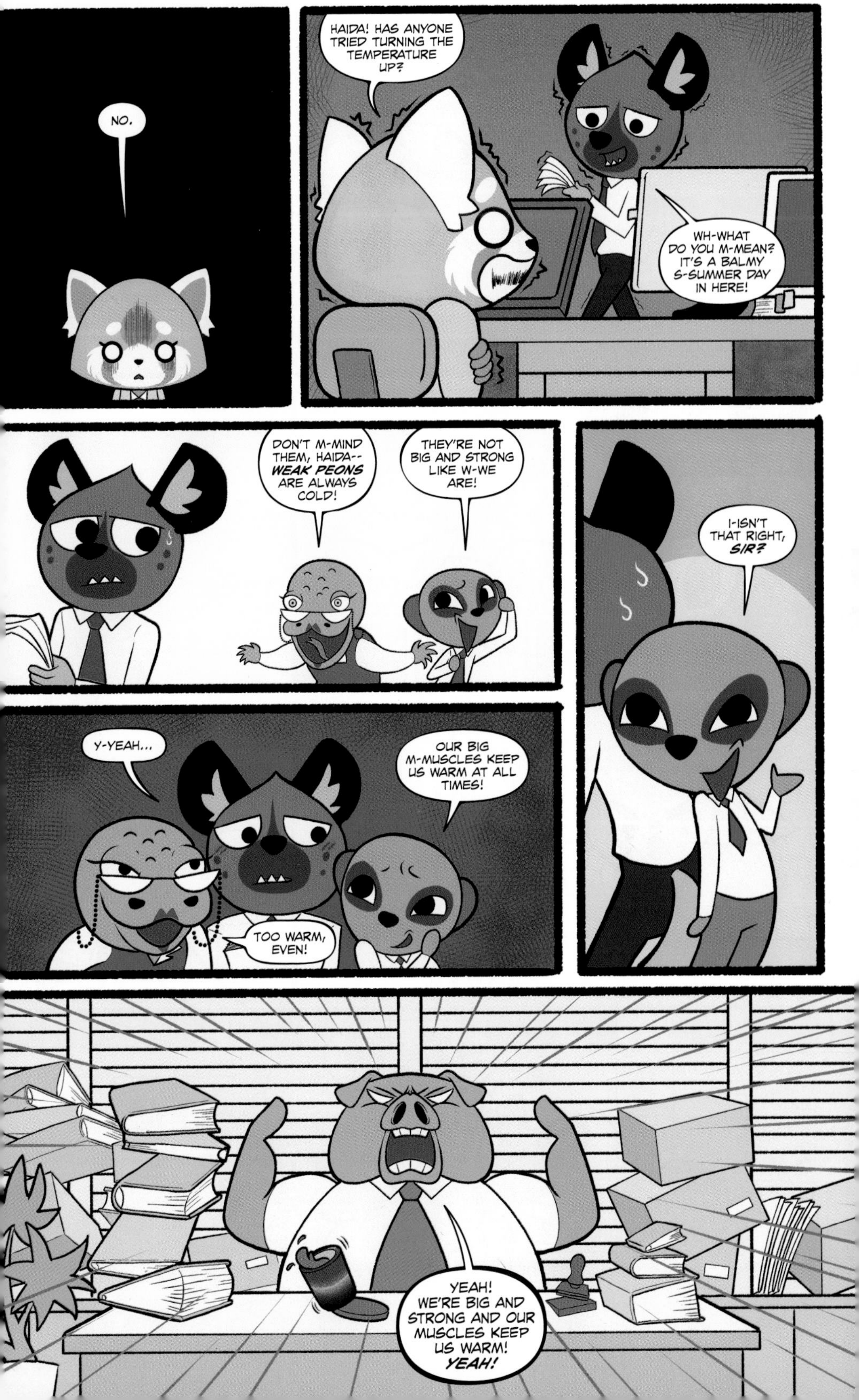
NO.
HAIDA! HAS ANYONE TRIED TURNING THE TEMPERATURE UP?
WH-WHAT DO YOU M-MEAN? IT'S A BALMY S-SUMMER DAY IN HERE!
DON'T M-MIND THEM, HAIDA-- WEAK PEONS ARE ALWAYS COLD!
THEY'RE NOT BIG AND STRONG LIKE W-WE ARE!
I-ISN'T THAT RIGHT, SIR?
Y-YEAH...
OUR BIG M-MUSCLES KEEP US WARM AT ALL TIMES!
TOO WARM, EVEN!
YEAH! WE'RE BIG AND STRONG AND OUR MUSCLES KEEP US WARM! YEAH!

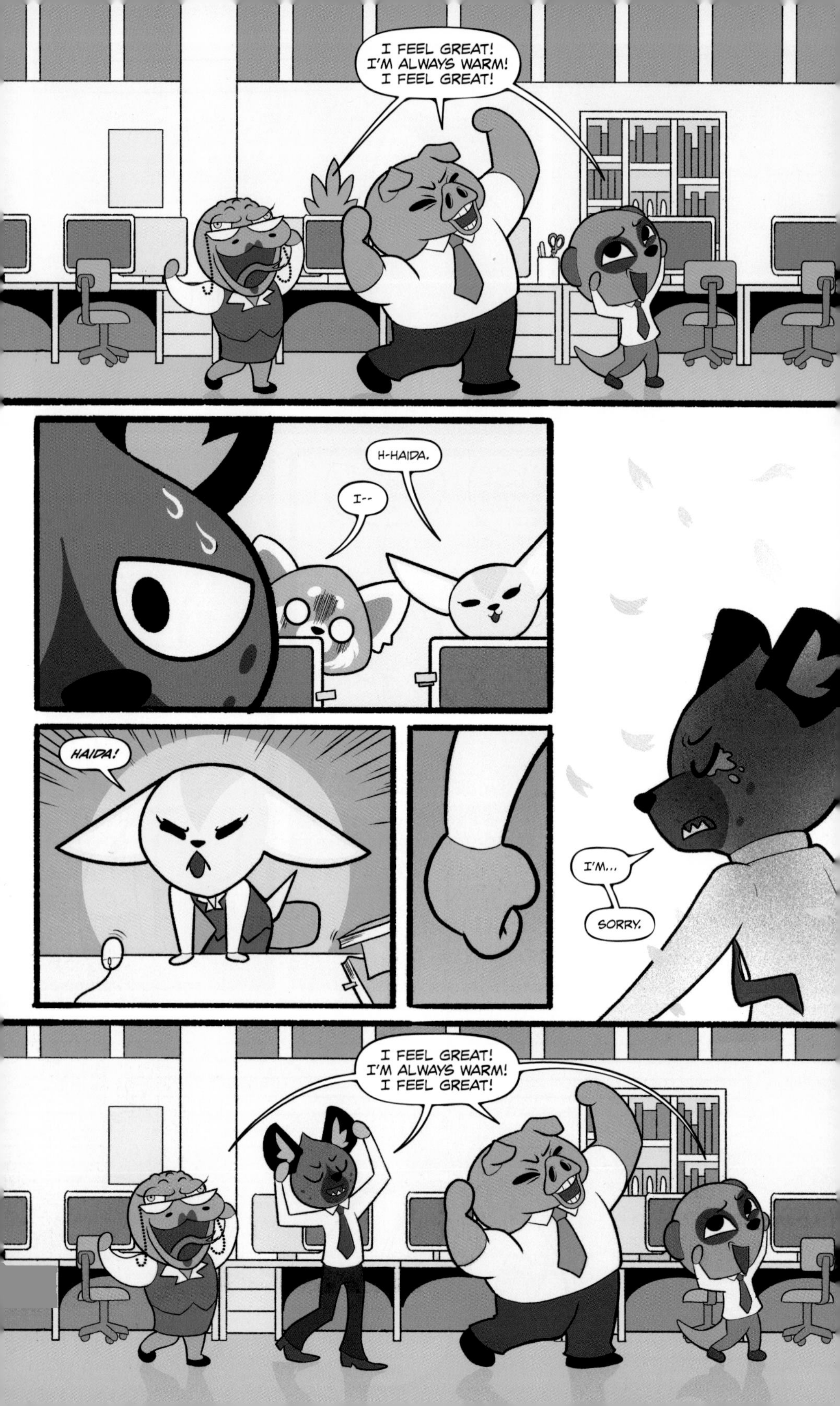
I FEEL GREAT!
I'M ALWAYS WARM!
I FEEL GREAT!
H-HAIDA.
I--
HAIDA!
I'M...
SORRY.
I FEEL GREAT!
I'M ALWAYS WARM!
I FEEL GREAT!

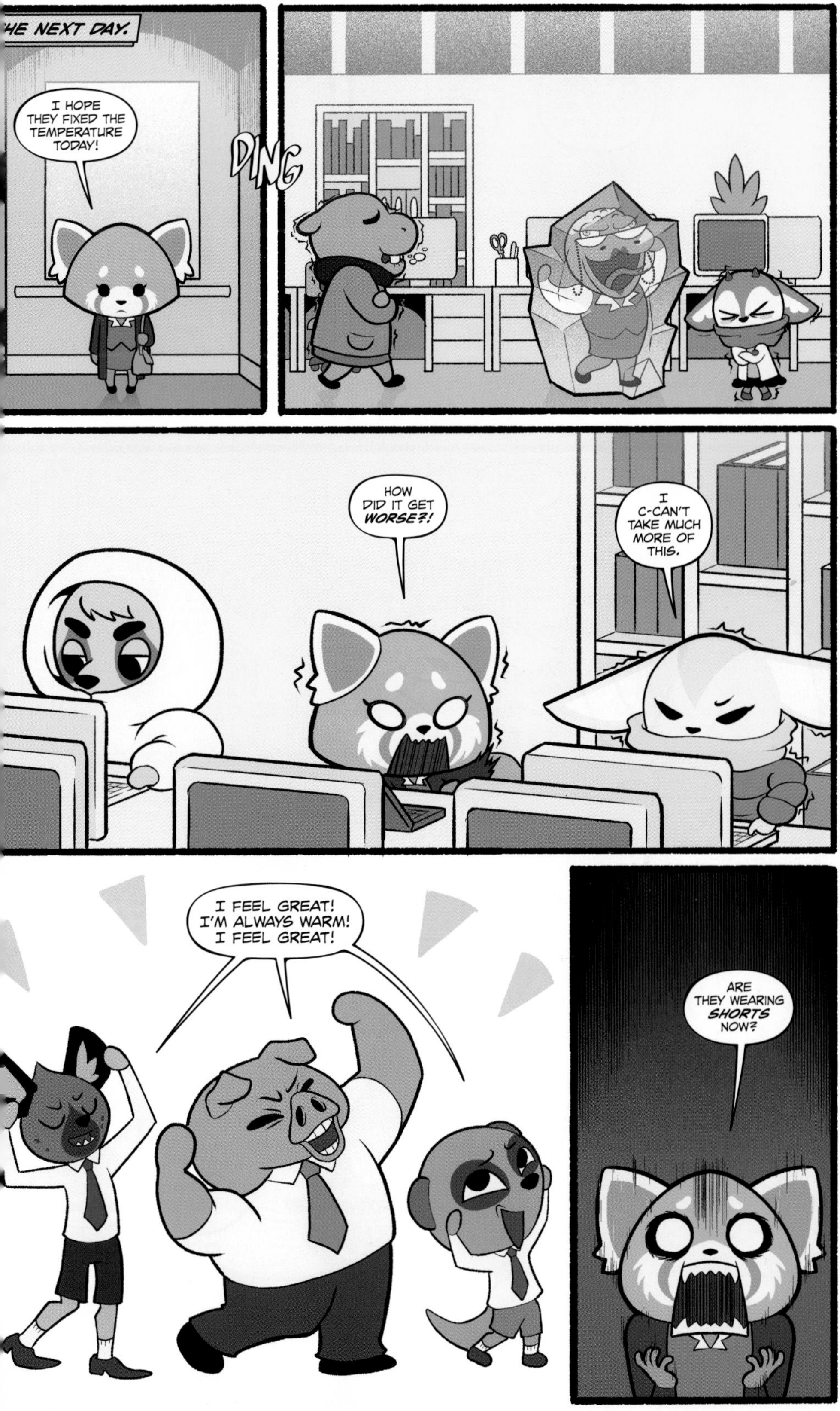

THE NEXT DAY.
I HOPE THEY FIXED THE TEMPERATURE TODAY!
DING
HOW DID IT GET *WORSE?!*
I C-CAN'T TAKE MUCH MORE OF THIS.
I FEEL GREAT! I'M ALWAYS WARM! I FEEL GREAT!
ARE THEY WEARING *SHORTS* NOW?

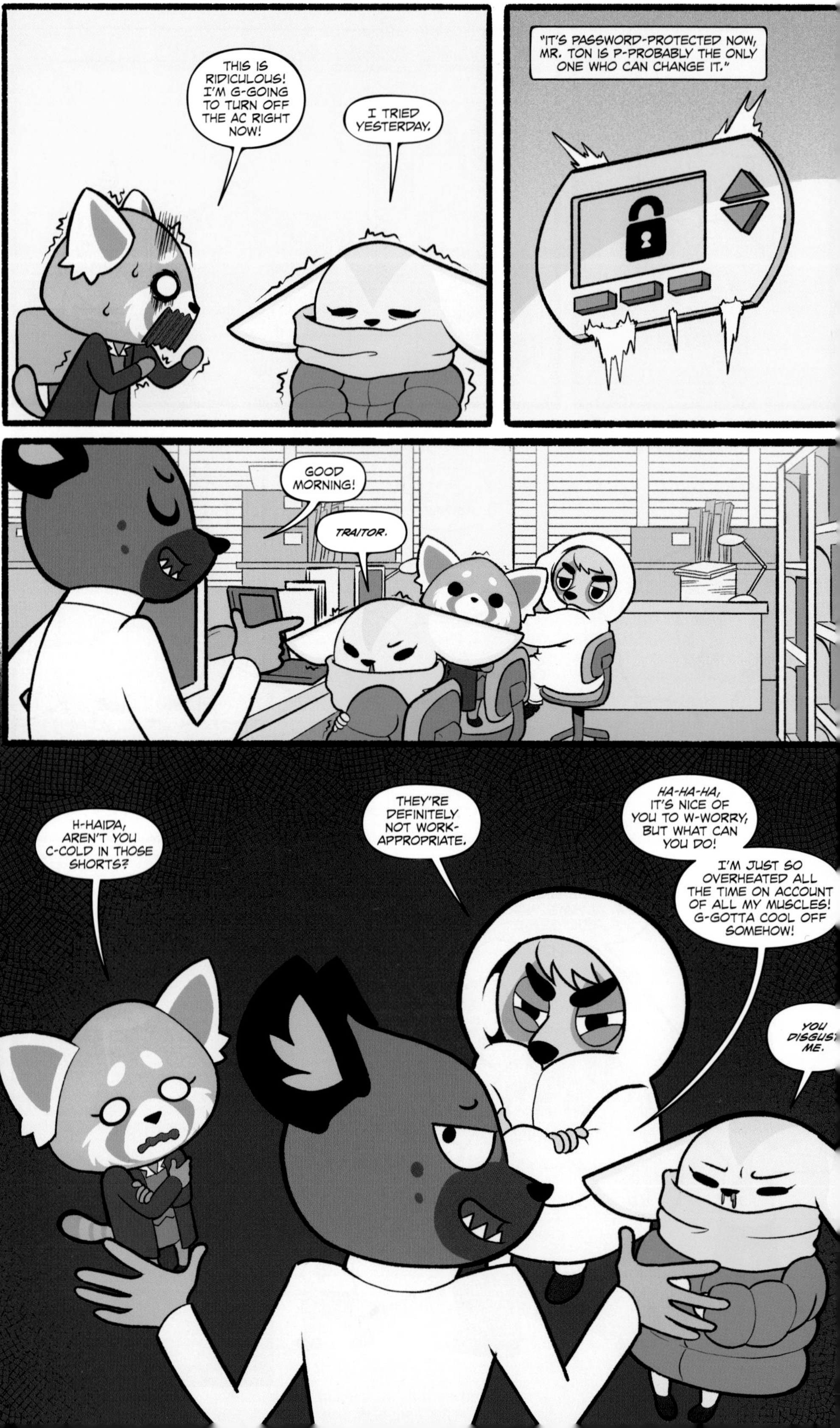

THIS IS RIDICULOUS! I'M G-GOING TO TURN OFF THE AC RIGHT NOW!
I TRIED YESTERDAY.
"IT'S PASSWORD-PROTECTED NOW, MR. TON IS P-PROBABLY THE ONLY ONE WHO CAN CHANGE IT."
GOOD MORNING!
TRAITOR.
H-HAIDA, AREN'T YOU C-COLD IN THOSE SHORTS?
THEY'RE DEFINITELY NOT WORK-APPROPRIATE.
HA-HA-HA, IT'S NICE OF YOU TO W-WORRY, BUT WHAT CAN YOU DO!
I'M JUST SO OVERHEATED ALL THE TIME ON ACCOUNT OF ALL MY MUSCLES! G-GOTTA COOL OFF SOMEHOW!
YOU DISGUST ME.

MY F-FINGERS ARE TOO COLD TO USE MY PHONE!

ANAI, Y-YOU'RE NOT COMING IN TO WORK WITH SHORTS T-TOMORROW, ARE YOU?

ABSOLUTELY N-NOT! PRETENDING YOU'RE O-OVERHEATED BY MUSCLES YOU DON'T HAVE IS...

..COMPLETELY REPULSIVE.

SO THIS IS THE COMPANY ICE AGE.

KRAKL KRAK

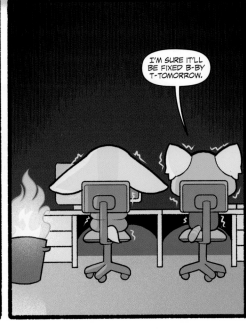

I'M SURE IT'LL BE FIXED B-BY T-TOMORROW.

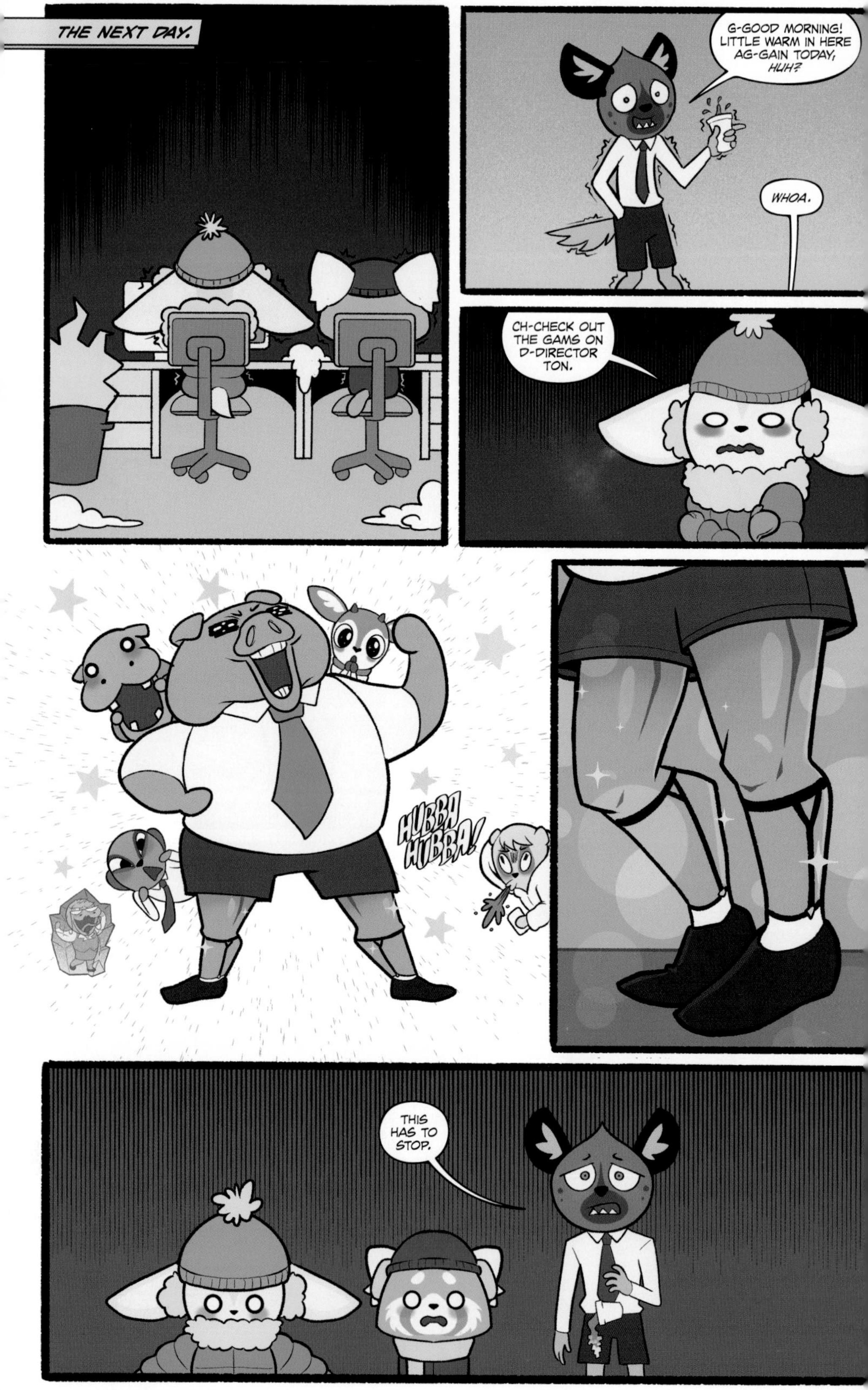
THE NEXT DAY.
G-GOOD MORNING! LITTLE WARM IN HERE AG-GAIN TODAY, HUH?
WHOA.
CH-CHECK OUT THE GAMS ON D-DIRECTOR TON.
HUBBA HUBBA!
THIS HAS TO STOP.

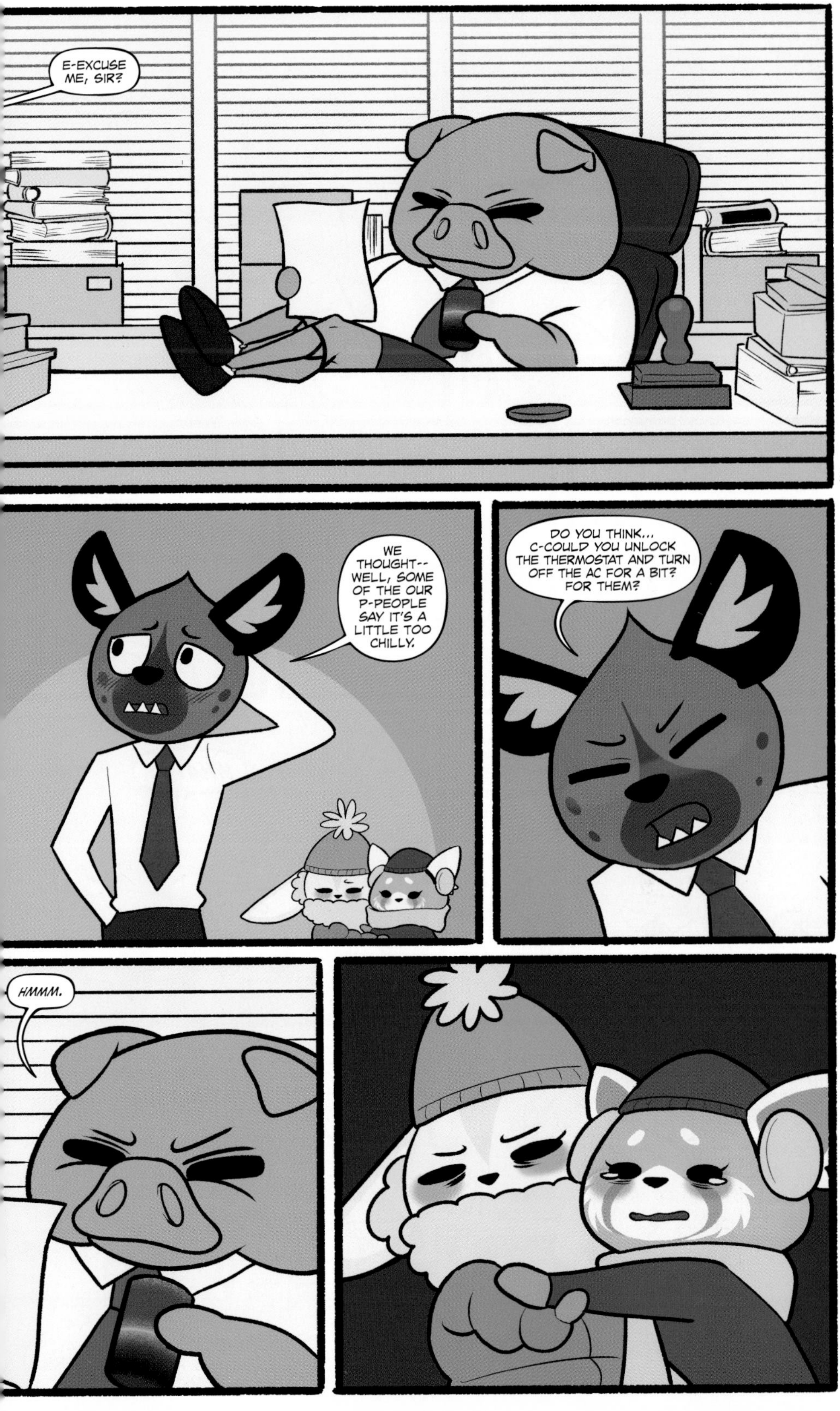
E-EXCUSE ME, SIR?
WE THOUGHT-- WELL, SOME OF THE OUR P-PEOPLE SAY IT'S A LITTLE TOO CHILLY.
DO YOU THINK... C-COULD YOU UNLOCK THE THERMOSTAT AND TURN OFF THE AC FOR A BIT? FOR THEM?
HMMM.

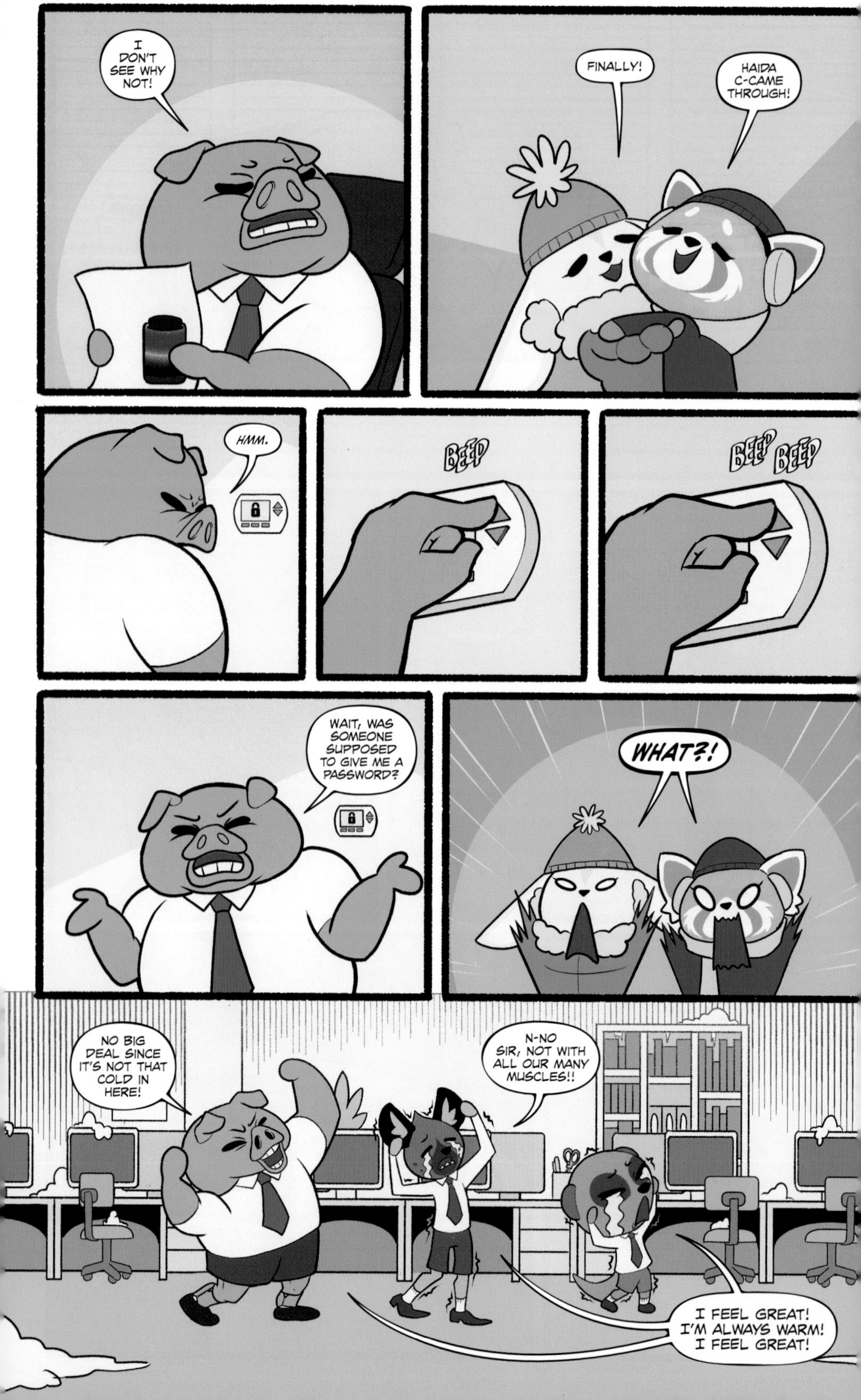
I DON'T SEE WHY NOT!
FINALLY!
HAIDA C-CAME THROUGH!
HMM.
BEEP
BEEP BEEP
WAIT, WAS SOMEONE SUPPOSED TO GIVE ME A PASSWORD?
WHAT?!
NO BIG DEAL SINCE IT'S NOT THAT COLD IN HERE!
N-NO SIR, NOT WITH ALL OUR MANY MUSCLES!!
I FEEL GREAT! I'M ALWAYS WARM! I FEEL GREAT!

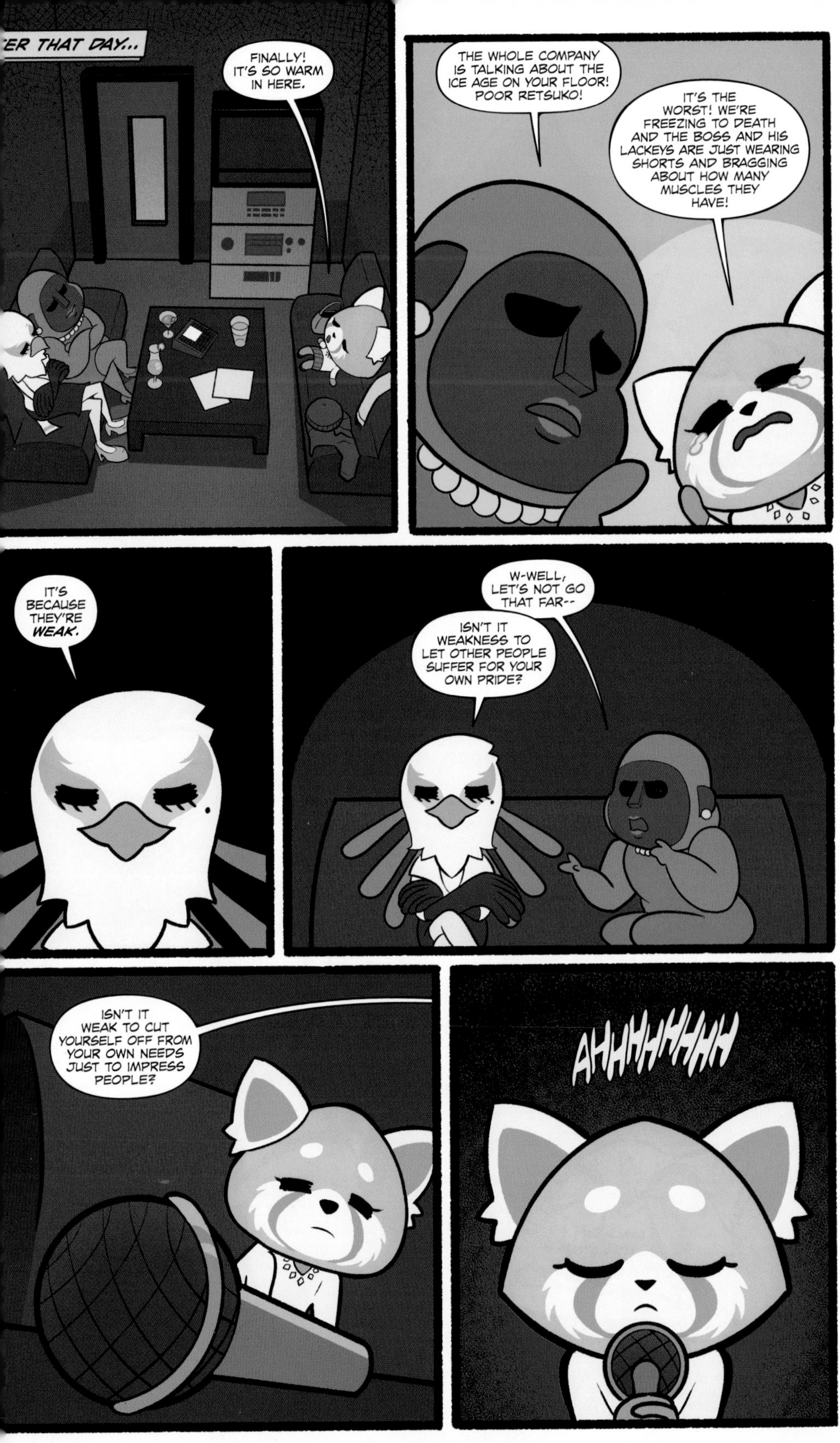
...ER THAT DAY...
FINALLY! IT'S SO WARM IN HERE.
THE WHOLE COMPANY IS TALKING ABOUT THE ICE AGE ON YOUR FLOOR! POOR RETSUKO!
IT'S THE WORST! WE'RE FREEZING TO DEATH AND THE BOSS AND HIS LACKEYS ARE JUST WEARING SHORTS AND BRAGGING ABOUT HOW MANY MUSCLES THEY HAVE!
IT'S BECAUSE THEY'RE *WEAK.*
W-WELL, LET'S NOT GO THAT FAR--
ISN'T IT WEAKNESS TO LET OTHER PEOPLE SUFFER FOR YOUR OWN PRIDE?
ISN'T IT WEAK TO CUT YOURSELF OFF FROM YOUR OWN NEEDS JUST TO IMPRESS PEOPLE?
AHHHHHHHH

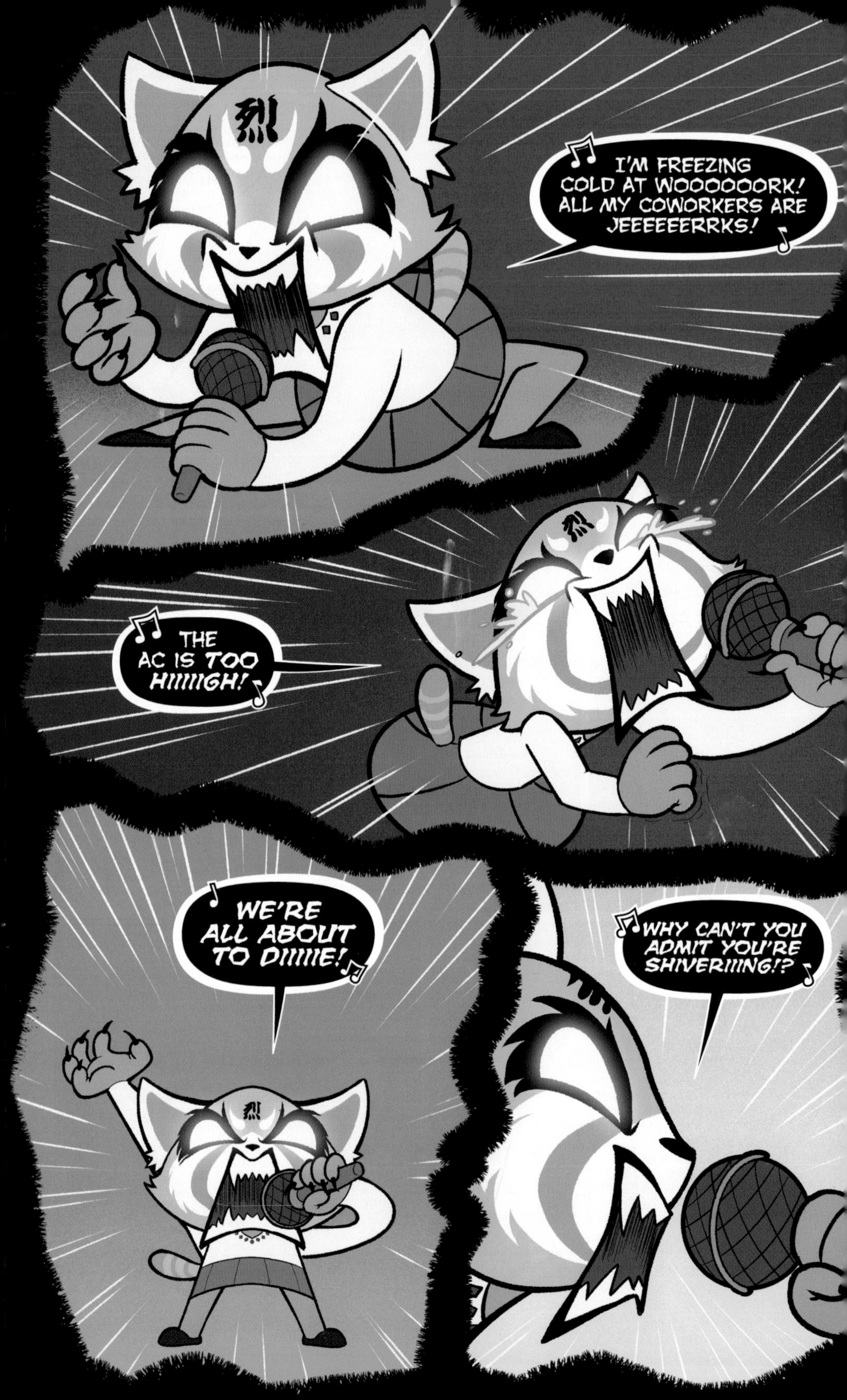
I'M FREEZING COLD AT WOOOOOORK! ALL MY COWORKERS ARE JEEEEEERRKS!
THE AC IS TOO HIIIIIGH!
WE'RE ALL ABOUT TO DIIIIIE!
WHY CAN'T YOU ADMIT YOU'RE SHIVERIIING!?

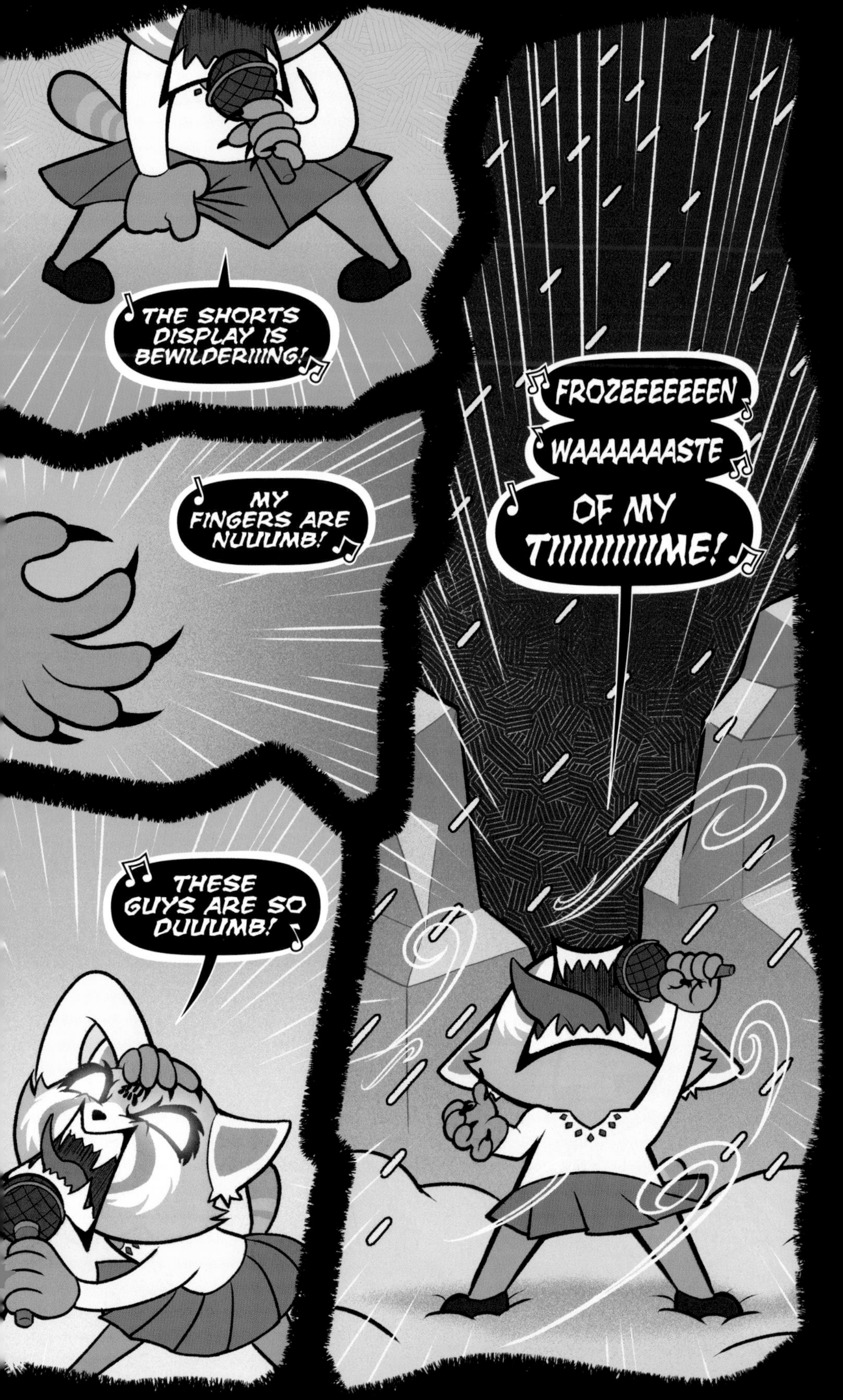
THE SHORTS DISPLAY IS BEWILDERIIING!
MY FINGERS ARE NUUUMB!
THESE GUYS ARE SO DUUUMB!
FROZEEEEEEEN WAAAAAAAASTE OF MY TIIIIIIIIIME!

VALID POINT.

WE NEED TO FOCUS ON WHAT'S IMPORTANT!

RETSUKO AND THE ACCOUNTANT WILL DIE IF THIS ISN'T SOLVED!

WASHIMI IS RIGHT! WE NEED TO FIGURE OUT HOW TO UNLOCK THE THERMOSTAT!

WE SHOULD FIND WHOEVER DID IT!

SOMEONE WHO WANTED THE TEMPERATURE TO BE UNREASONABLY COLD.

AND WHO HAS ACCESS TO THE AIR-CONDITIONING SYSTEM ABOVE EVEN MR. TON!

AH! I KNOW WHO IT WAS!

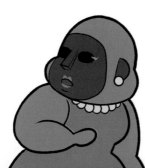

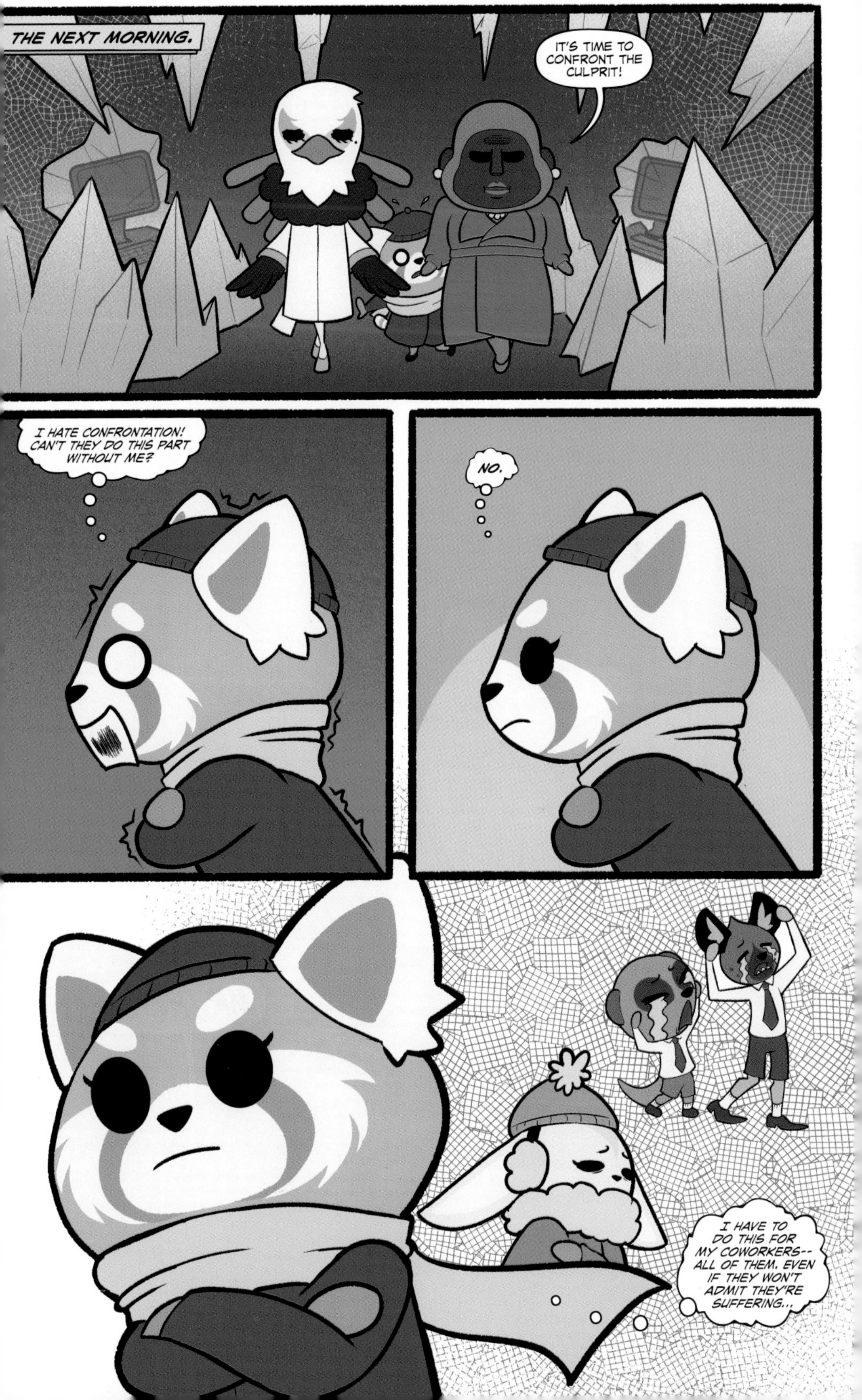
THE NEXT MORNING.
IT'S TIME TO CONFRONT THE CULPRIT!
I HATE CONFRONTATION! CAN'T THEY DO THIS PART WITHOUT ME?
NO.
I HAVE TO DO THIS FOR MY COWORKERS-- ALL OF THEM. EVEN IF THEY WON'T ADMIT THEY'RE SUFFERING...

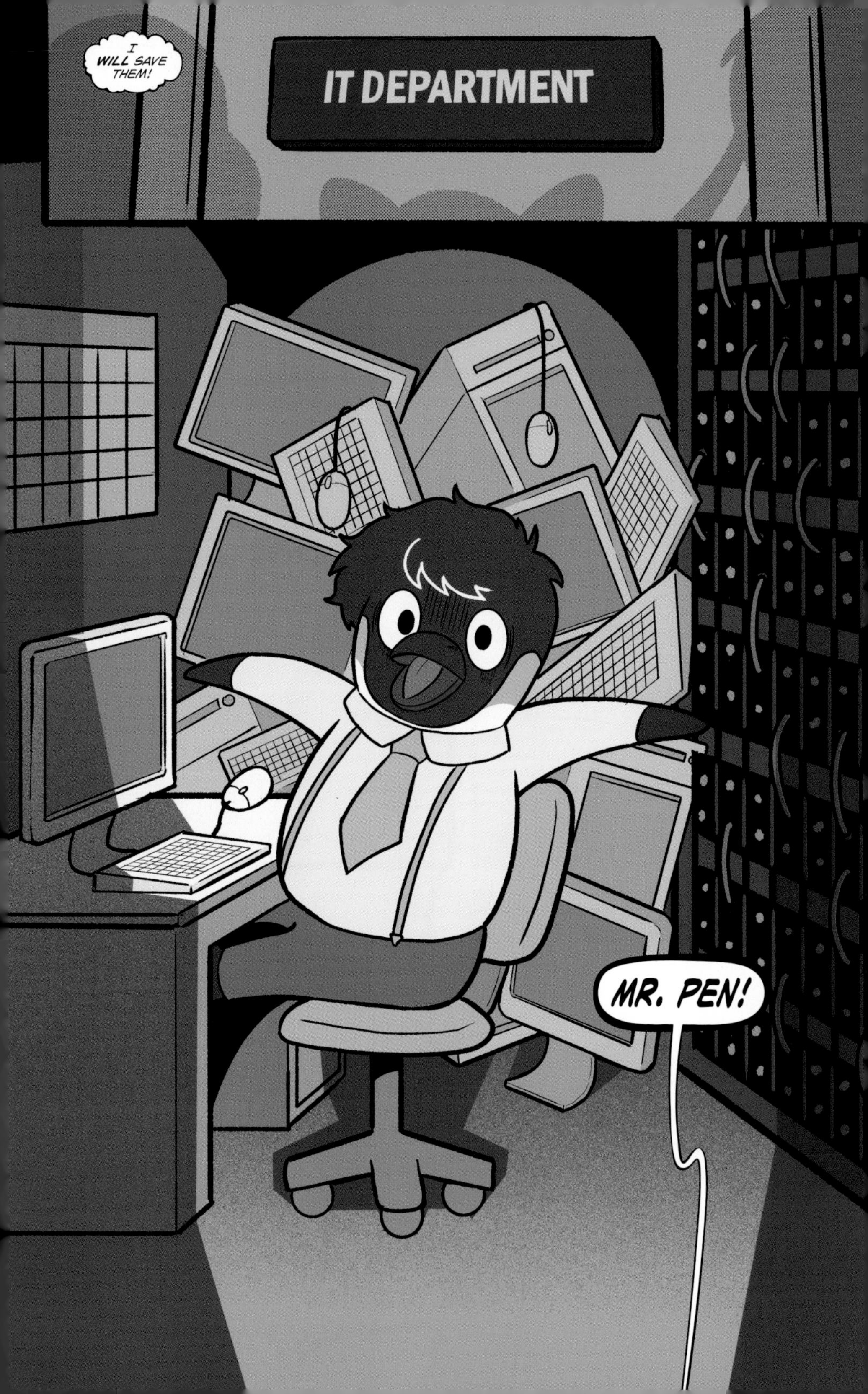
I WILL SAVE THEM!
IT DEPARTMENT
MR. PEN!

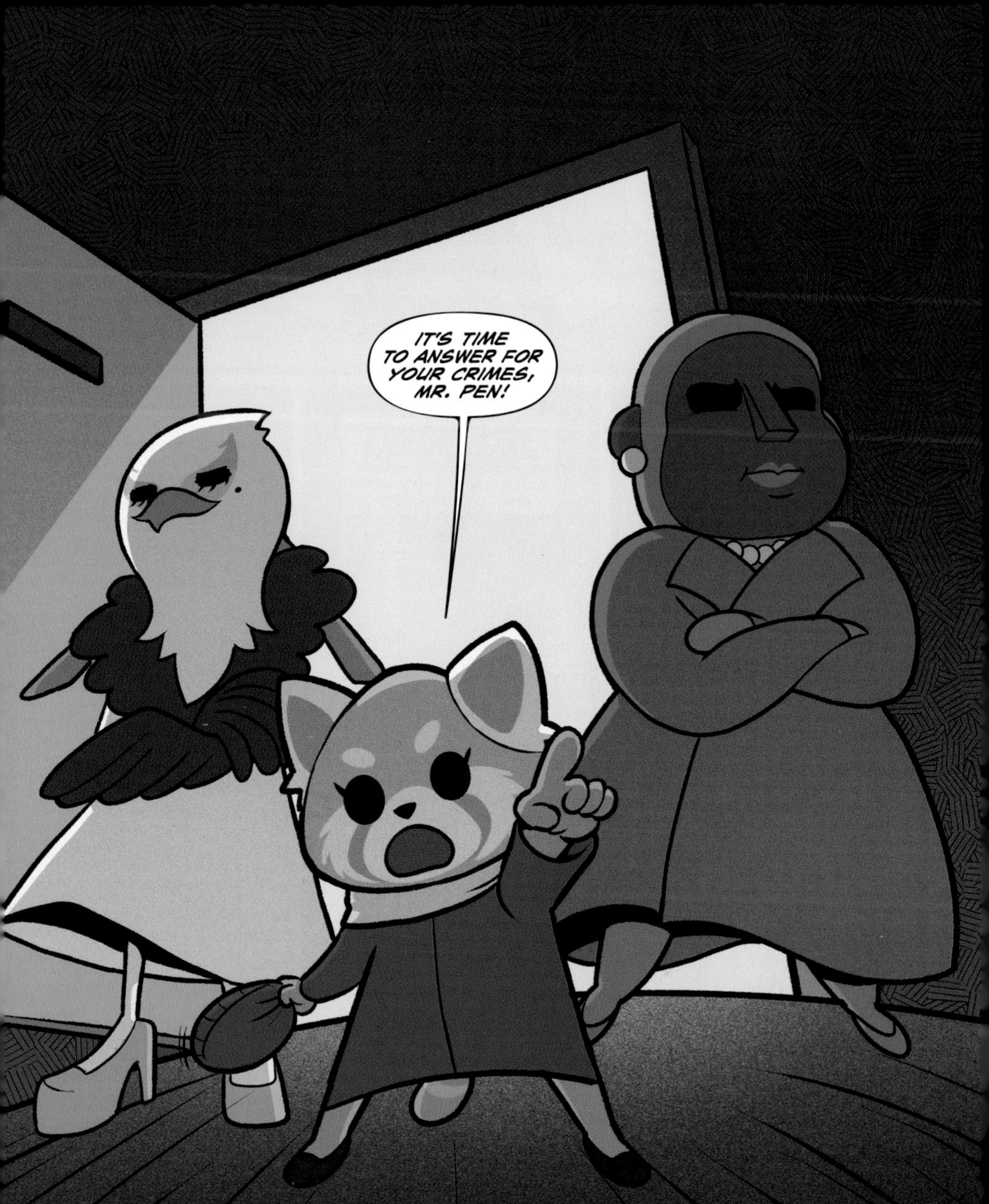
IT'S TIME TO ANSWER FOR YOUR CRIMES, MR. PEN!

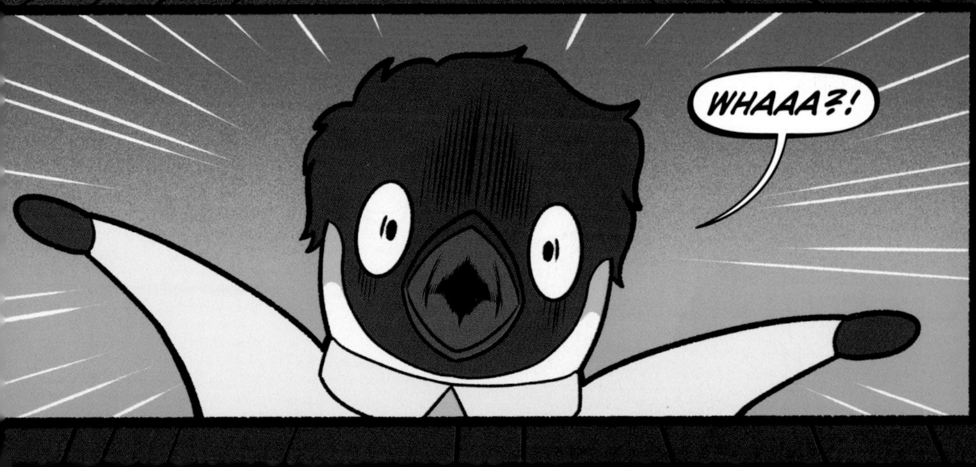
WHAAA?!

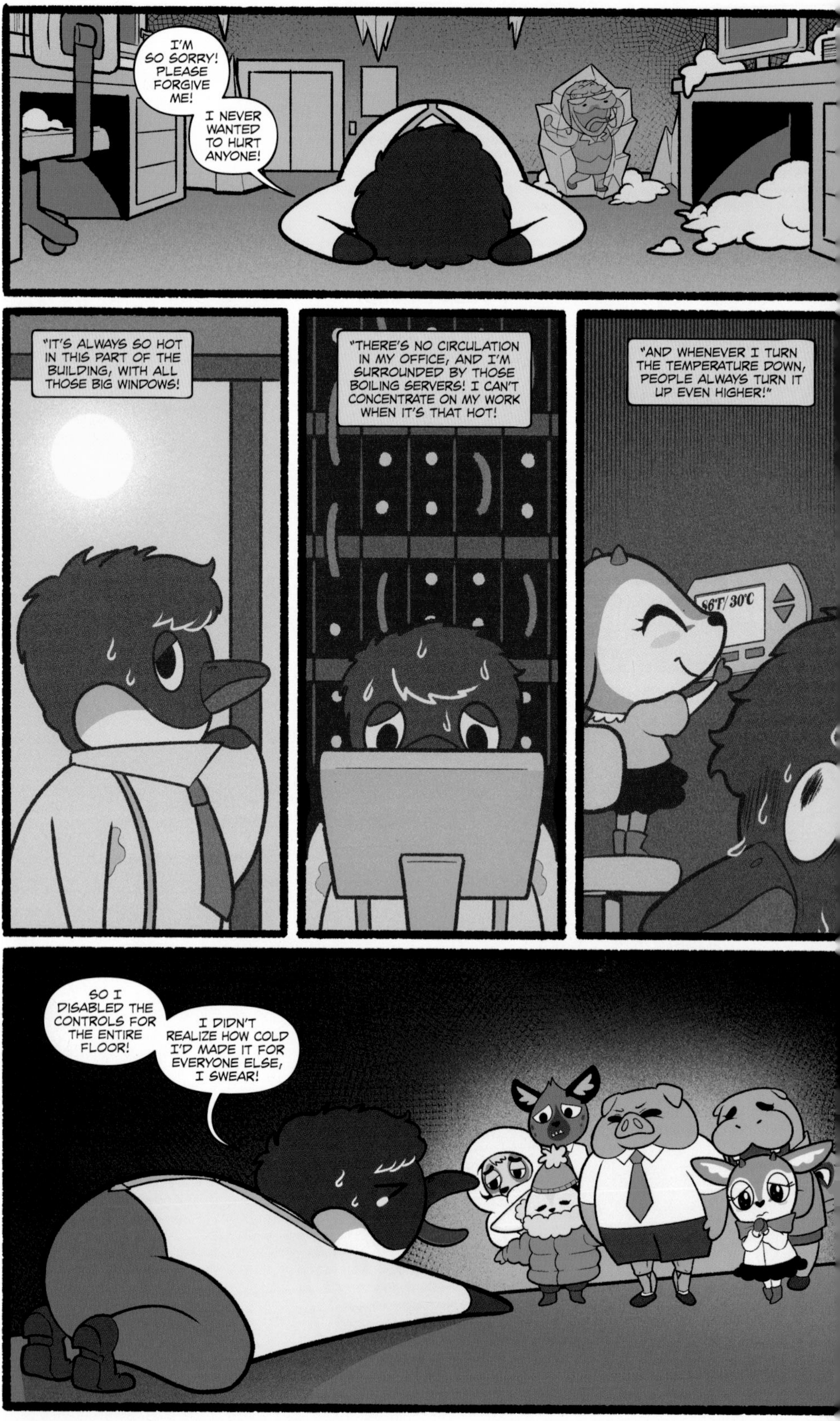
I'M SO SORRY! PLEASE FORGIVE ME!
I NEVER WANTED TO HURT ANYONE!
"IT'S ALWAYS SO HOT IN THIS PART OF THE BUILDING, WITH ALL THOSE BIG WINDOWS!
"THERE'S NO CIRCULATION IN MY OFFICE, AND I'M SURROUNDED BY THOSE BOILING SERVERS! I CAN'T CONCENTRATE ON MY WORK WHEN IT'S THAT HOT!
"AND WHENEVER I TURN THE TEMPERATURE DOWN, PEOPLE ALWAYS TURN IT UP EVEN HIGHER!"
86°F/30°C
SO I DISABLED THE CONTROLS FOR THE ENTIRE FLOOR!
I DIDN'T REALIZE HOW COLD I'D MADE IT FOR EVERYONE ELSE, I SWEAR!

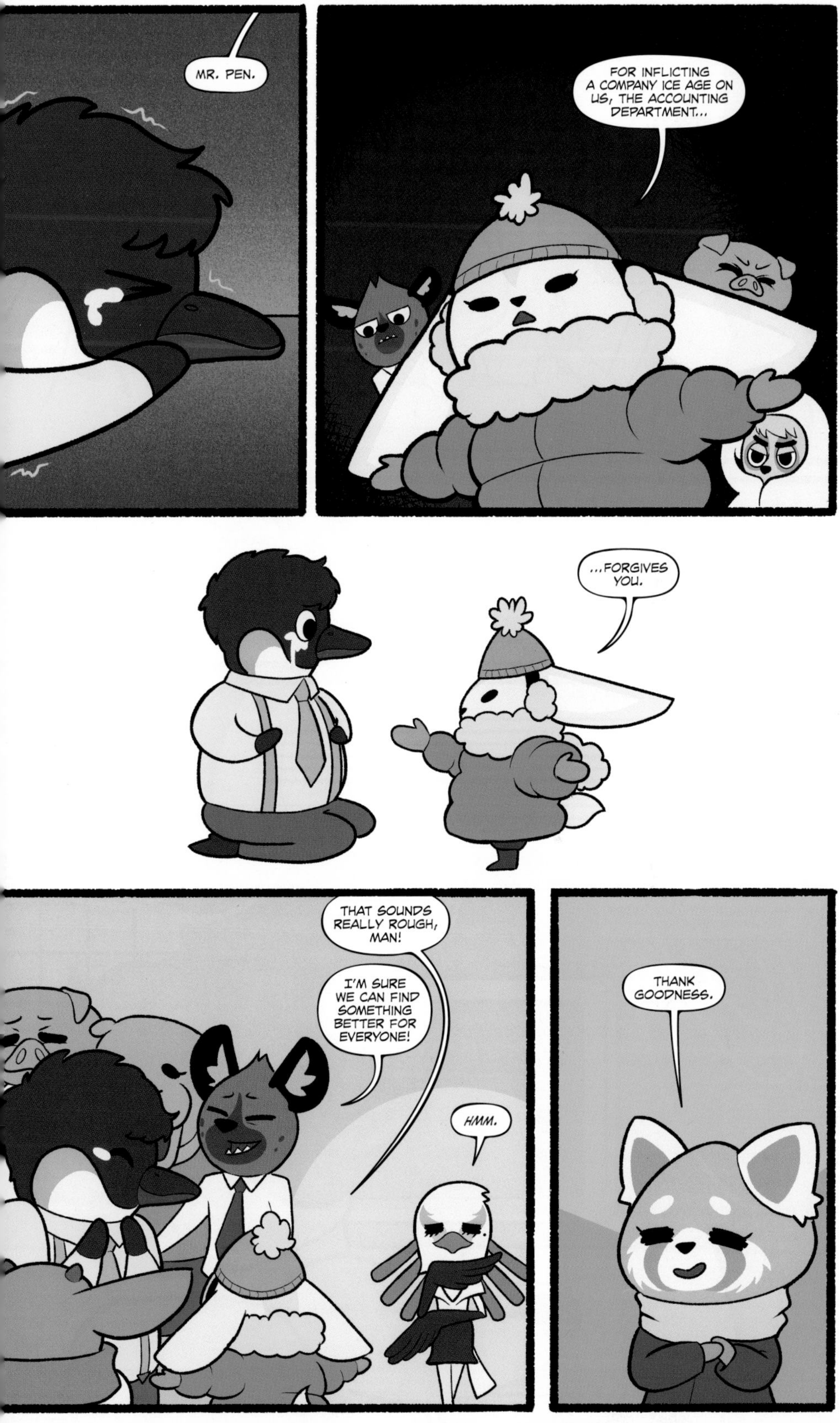
MR. PEN.
FOR INFLICTING A COMPANY ICE AGE ON US, THE ACCOUNTING DEPARTMENT...
...FORGIVES YOU.
THAT SOUNDS REALLY ROUGH, MAN!
I'M SURE WE CAN FIND SOMETHING BETTER FOR EVERYONE!
HMM.
THANK GOODNESS.

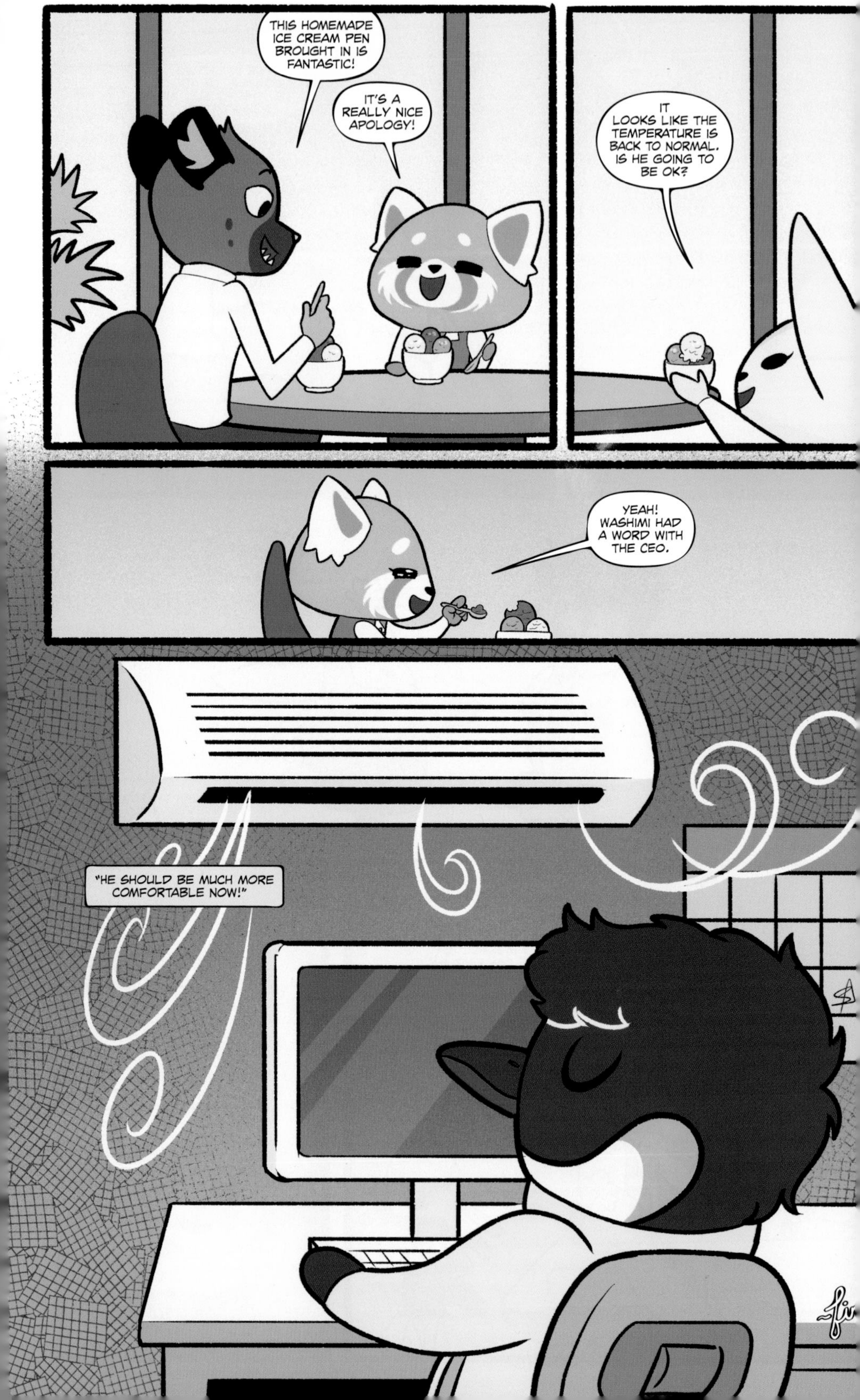
THIS HOMEMADE ICE CREAM PEN BROUGHT IN IS FANTASTIC!
IT'S A REALLY NICE APOLOGY!
IT LOOKS LIKE THE TEMPERATURE IS BACK TO NORMAL. IS HE GOING TO BE OK?
YEAH! WASHIMI HAD A WORD WITH THE CEO.
"HE SHOULD BE MUCH MORE COMFORTABLE NOW!"

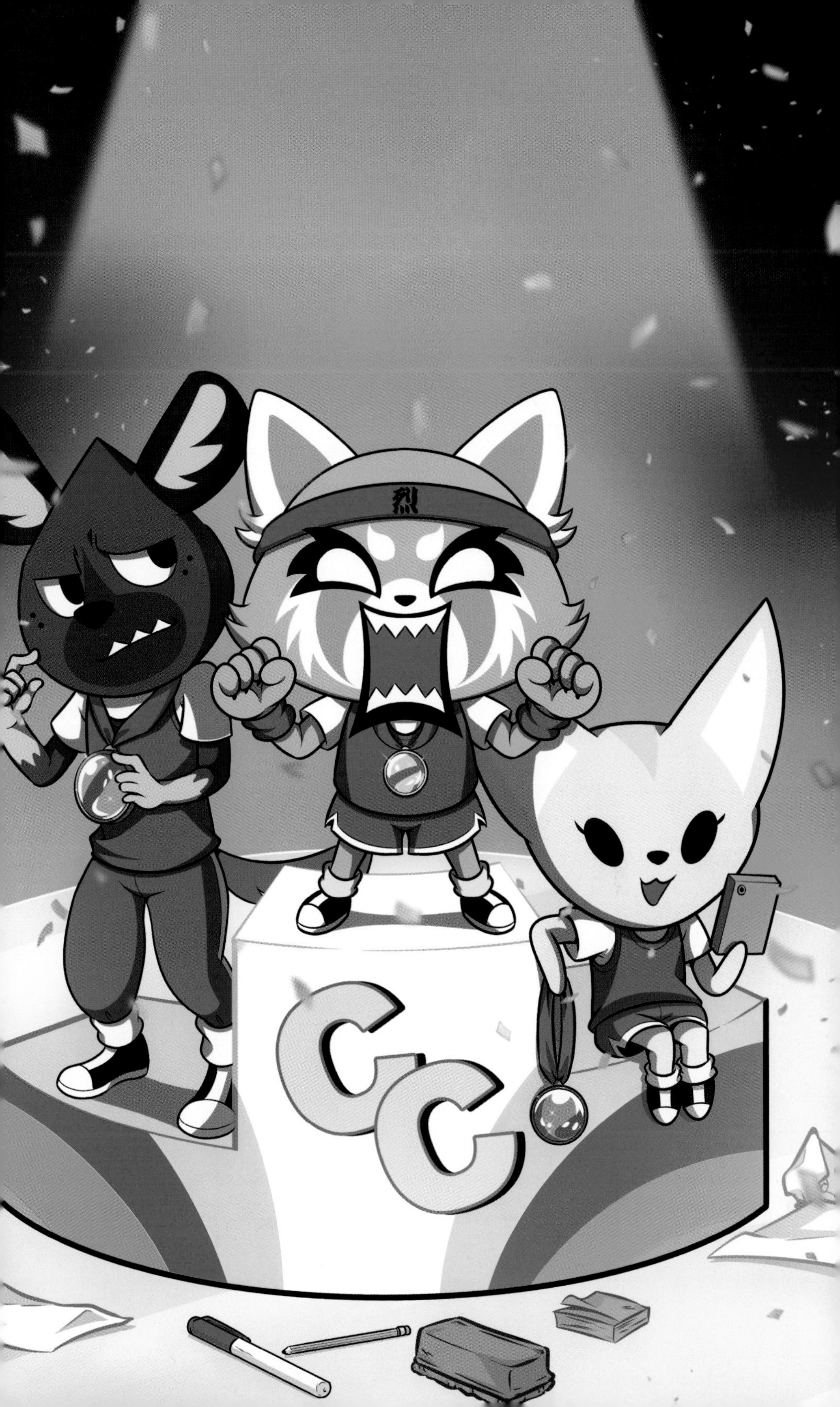
烈
CC

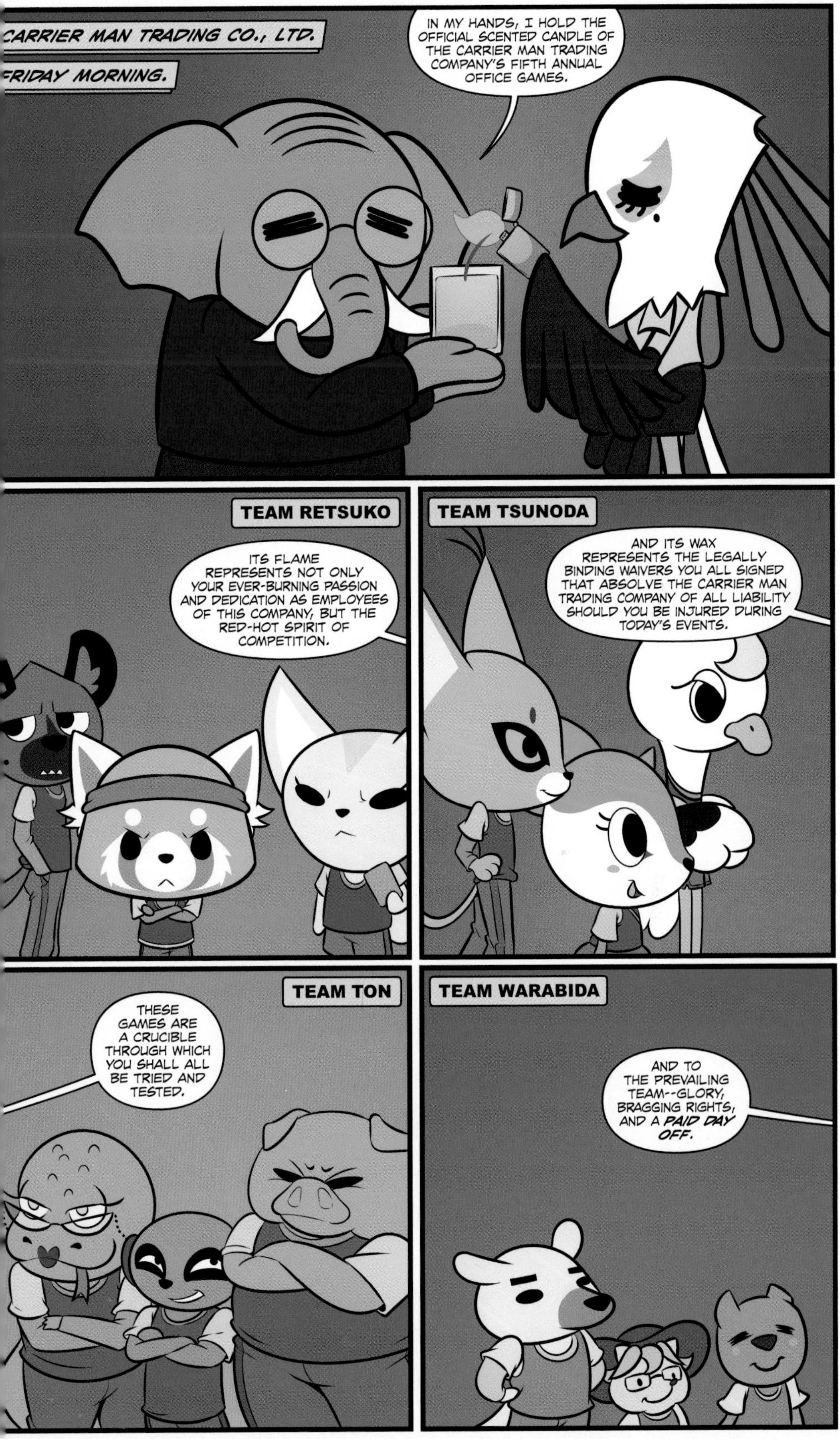

CARRIER MAN TRADING CO., LTD.
FRIDAY MORNING.
IN MY HANDS, I HOLD THE OFFICIAL SCENTED CANDLE OF THE CARRIER MAN TRADING COMPANY'S FIFTH ANNUAL OFFICE GAMES.
TEAM RETSUKO
ITS FLAME REPRESENTS NOT ONLY YOUR EVER-BURNING PASSION AND DEDICATION AS EMPLOYEES OF THIS COMPANY; BUT THE RED-HOT SPIRIT OF COMPETITION.
TEAM TSUNODA
AND ITS WAX REPRESENTS THE LEGALLY BINDING WAIVERS YOU ALL SIGNED THAT ABSOLVE THE CARRIER MAN TRADING COMPANY OF ALL LIABILITY SHOULD YOU BE INJURED DURING TODAY'S EVENTS.
TEAM TON
THESE GAMES ARE A CRUCIBLE THROUGH WHICH YOU SHALL ALL BE TRIED AND TESTED.
TEAM WARABIDA
AND TO THE PREVAILING TEAM--GLORY, BRAGGING RIGHTS, AND A PAID DAY OFF.

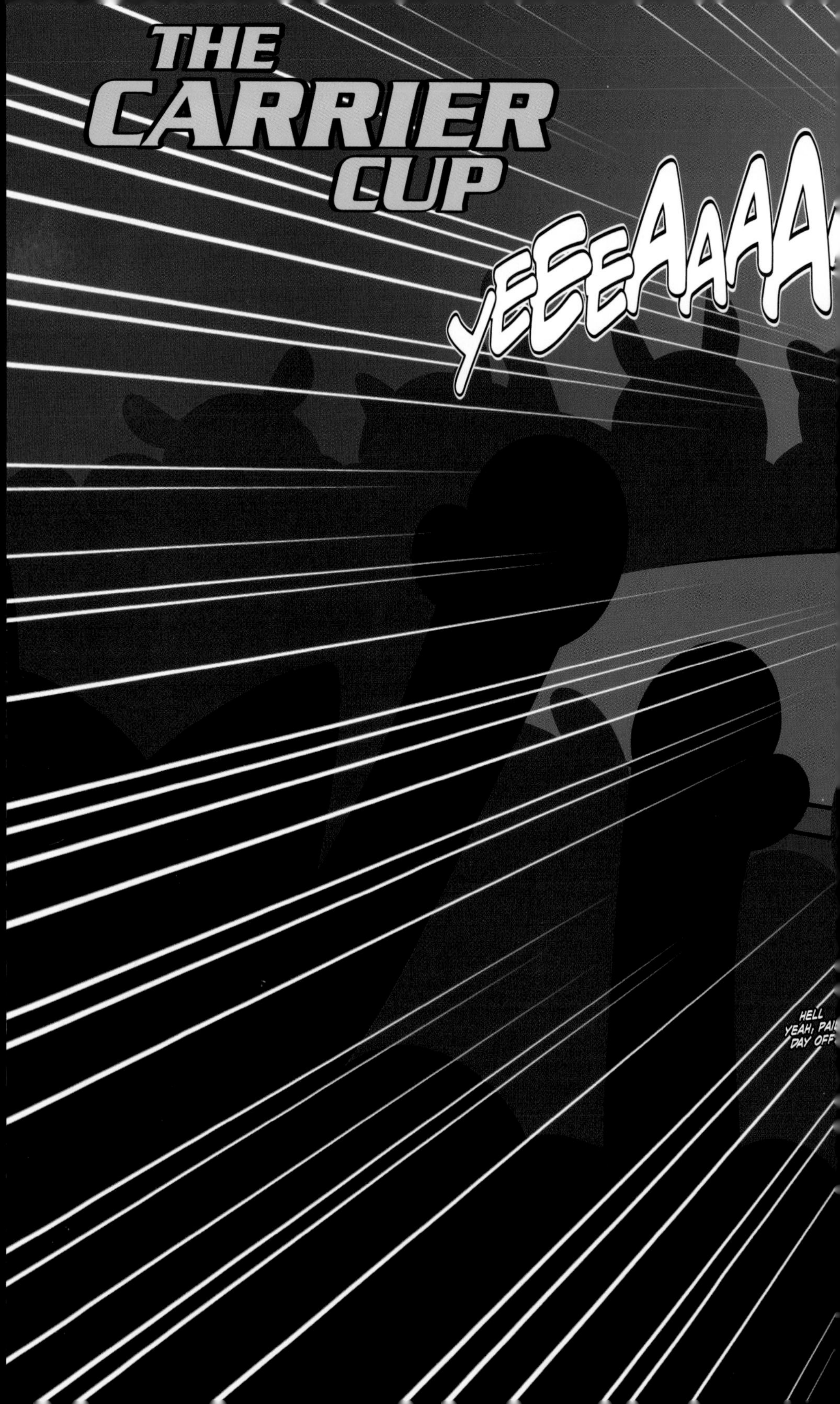
THE CARRIER CUP
YEEEEAAAA
HELL YEAH, PAI DAY OFF

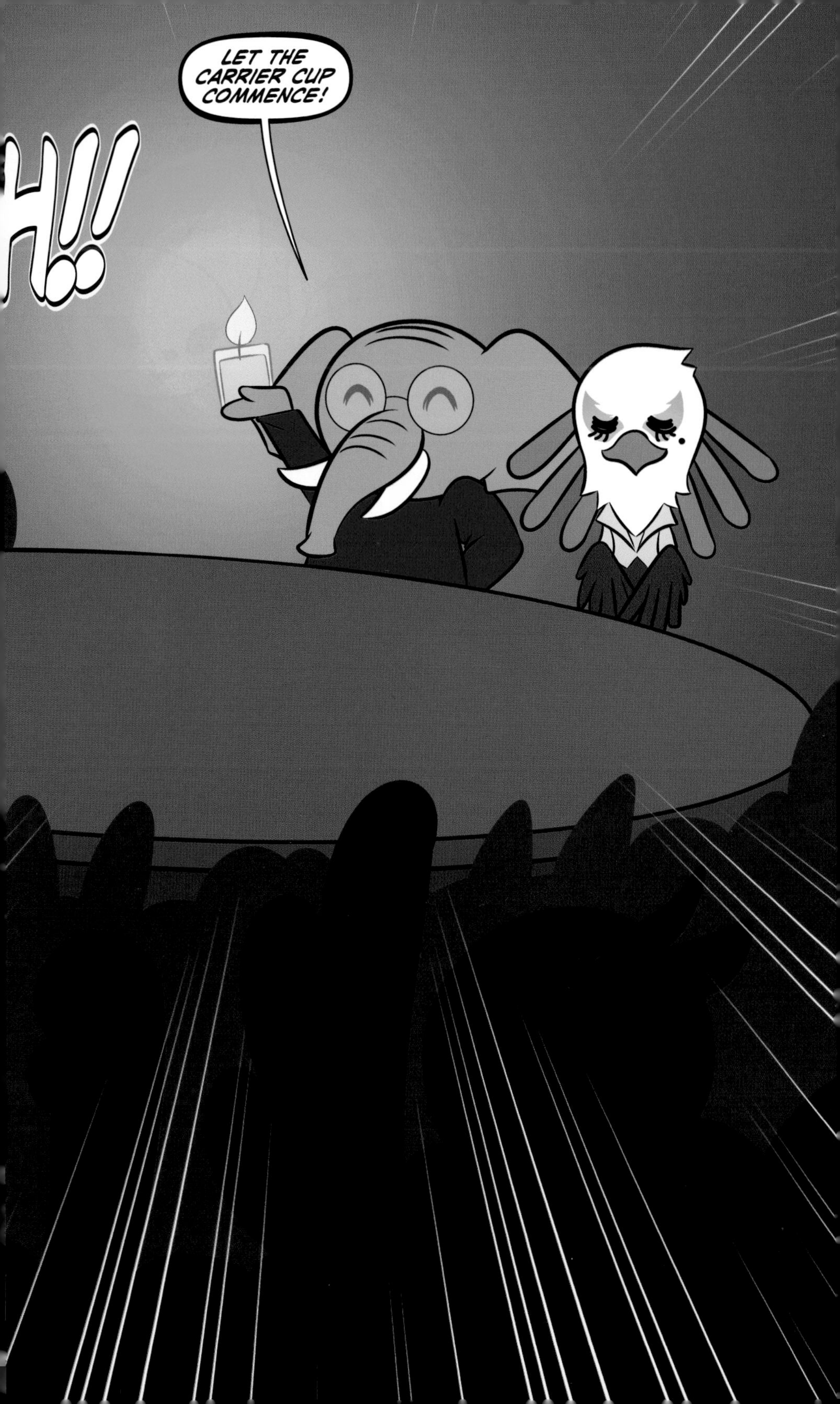
H!!
LET THE CARRIER CUP COMMENCE!

ALL RIGHT, GUYS. LAST YEAR MAY HAVE BEEN PRETTY ROUGH, BUT THIS YEAR WE'RE TAKING HOME THE GOLD FOR SURE!

THE ONLY THING SWEETER THAN THE BLOOD OF MY ENEMIES IS GETTING PAID TO NOT SHOW UP TO THIS DUMP FOR A DAY.

THAT'S THE SPIR NOW BR. IT IN!

"DAY OFF" ON THREE!

ONE... TWO...

DAY OFF!

RETSUKO SURE IS CUTE WHEN SHE'S FIRED UP...

OH-EM-GEE, THAT'S SOOO ADORABLE!

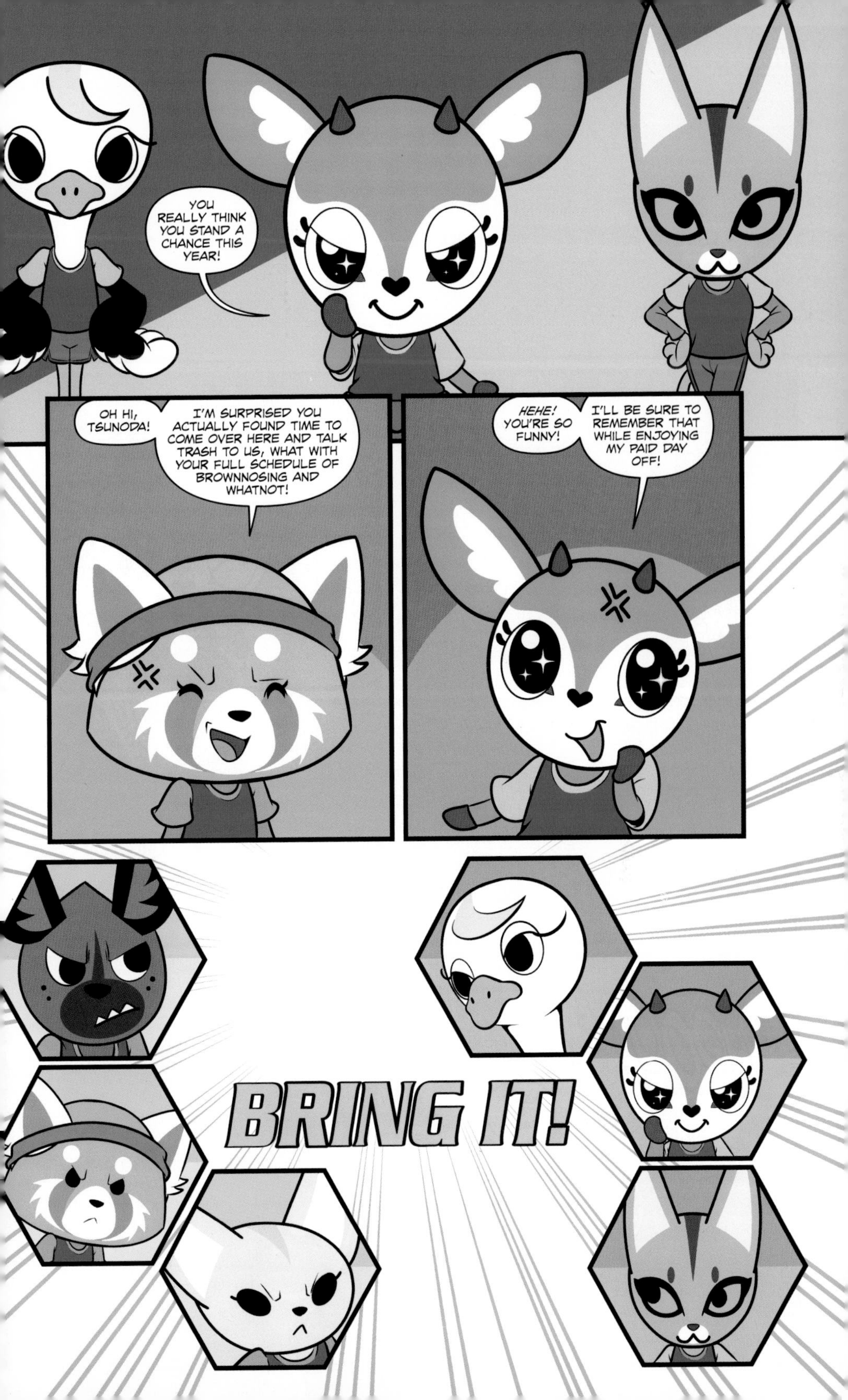
YOU REALLY THINK YOU STAND A CHANCE THIS YEAR!
OH HI, TSUNODA!
I'M SURPRISED YOU ACTUALLY FOUND TIME TO COME OVER HERE AND TALK TRASH TO US, WHAT WITH YOUR FULL SCHEDULE OF BROWNNOSING AND WHATNOT!
HEHE! YOU'RE SO FUNNY!
I'LL BE SURE TO REMEMBER THAT WHILE ENJOYING MY PAID DAY OFF!
BRING IT!

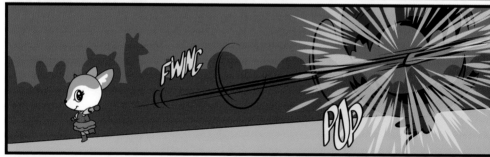

FWING

POP

WHOOOAAAAAa!

HEHE! TOO EASY!

TEAM TSUNODA WINS!

SUCK IT, RETSUKO!

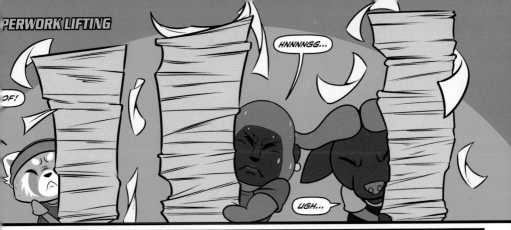

HNNNNNGG...

UGH...

COME ON, RETSUKO! DIG DOWN DEEP!

THINK ABOUT THE DAY OFF!

GRRRRRRR

RRRAAAAAHHH!!

TEAM RETSUKO WINS!

THAT WAS NOTHING COMPARED TO THE MOUNTAINS OF PAPERWORK TSUBONE'S PAWNED OFF ON ME.

PHEW!

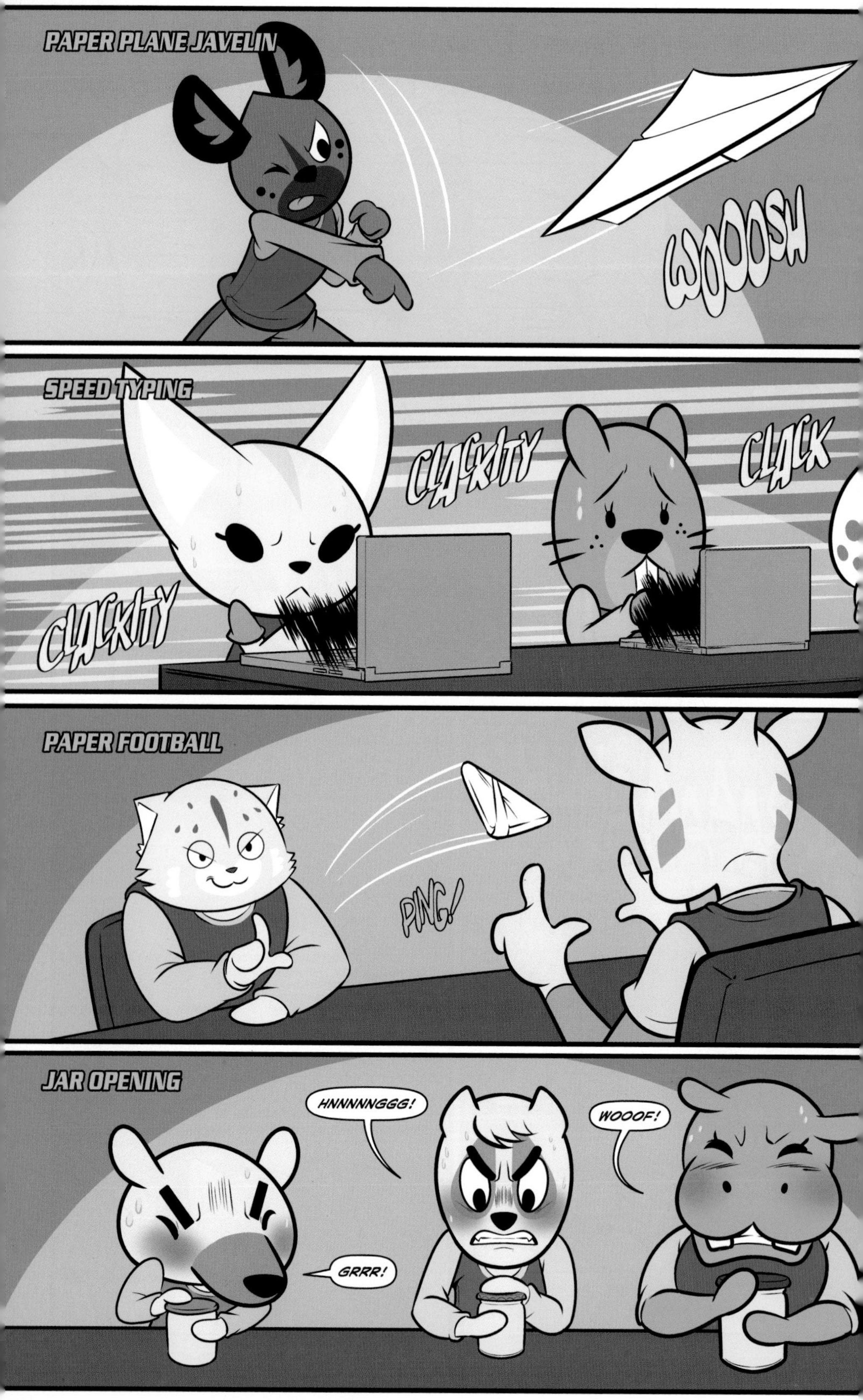
PAPER PLANE JAVELIN
WOOOSH
SPEED TYPING
CLACKITY
CLACKITY
CLACK
PAPER FOOTBALL
PING!
JAR OPENING
HNNNNNGGG!
WOOOF!
GRRR!

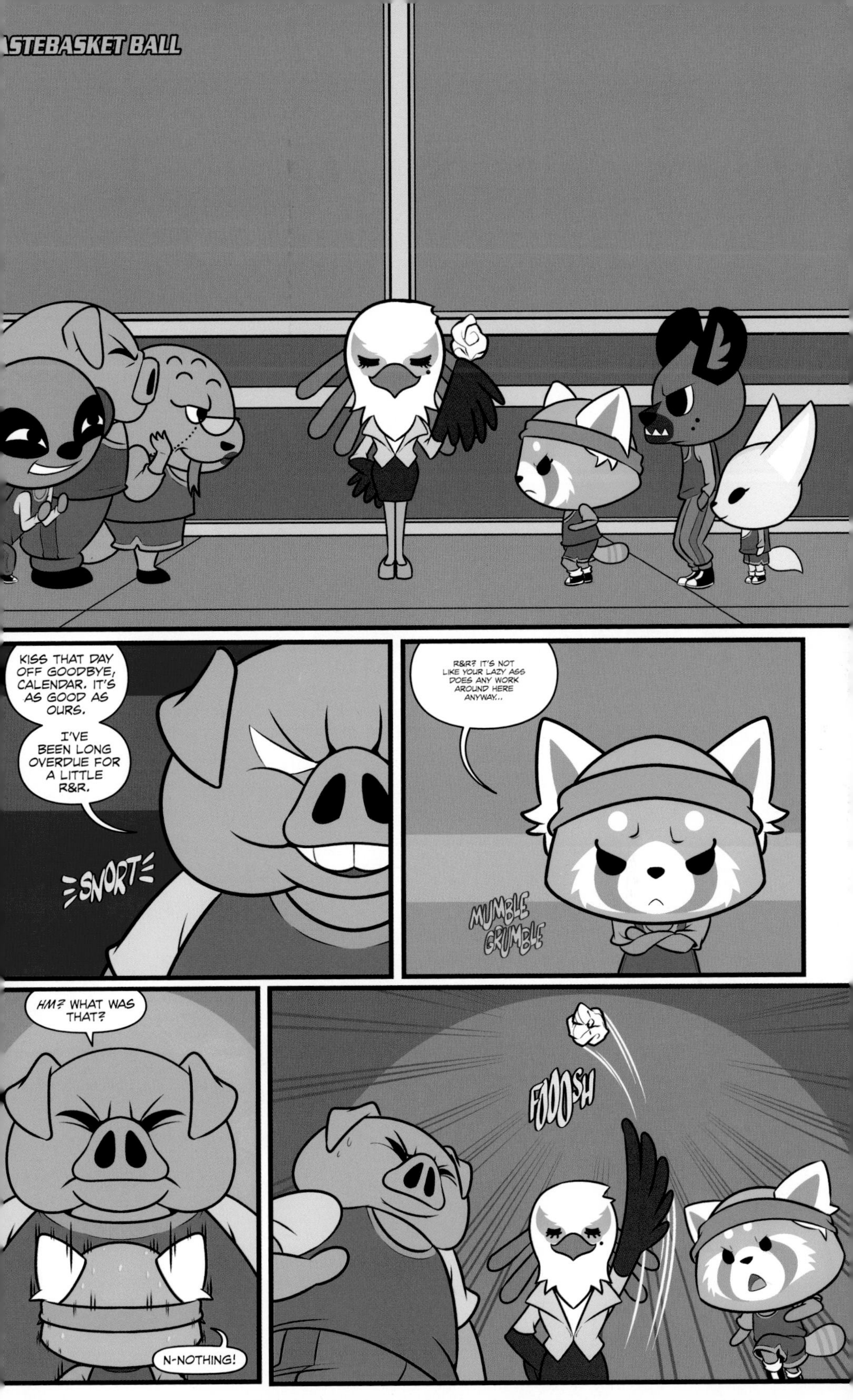
KISS THAT DAY OFF GOODBYE, CALENDAR. IT'S AS GOOD AS OURS.
I'VE BEEN LONG OVERDUE FOR A LITTLE R&R.
SNORT
R&R? IT'S NOT LIKE YOUR LAZY ASS DOES ANY WORK AROUND HERE ANYWAY...
MUMBLE GRUMBLE
HM? WHAT WAS THAT?
N-NOTHING!
FOOOSH

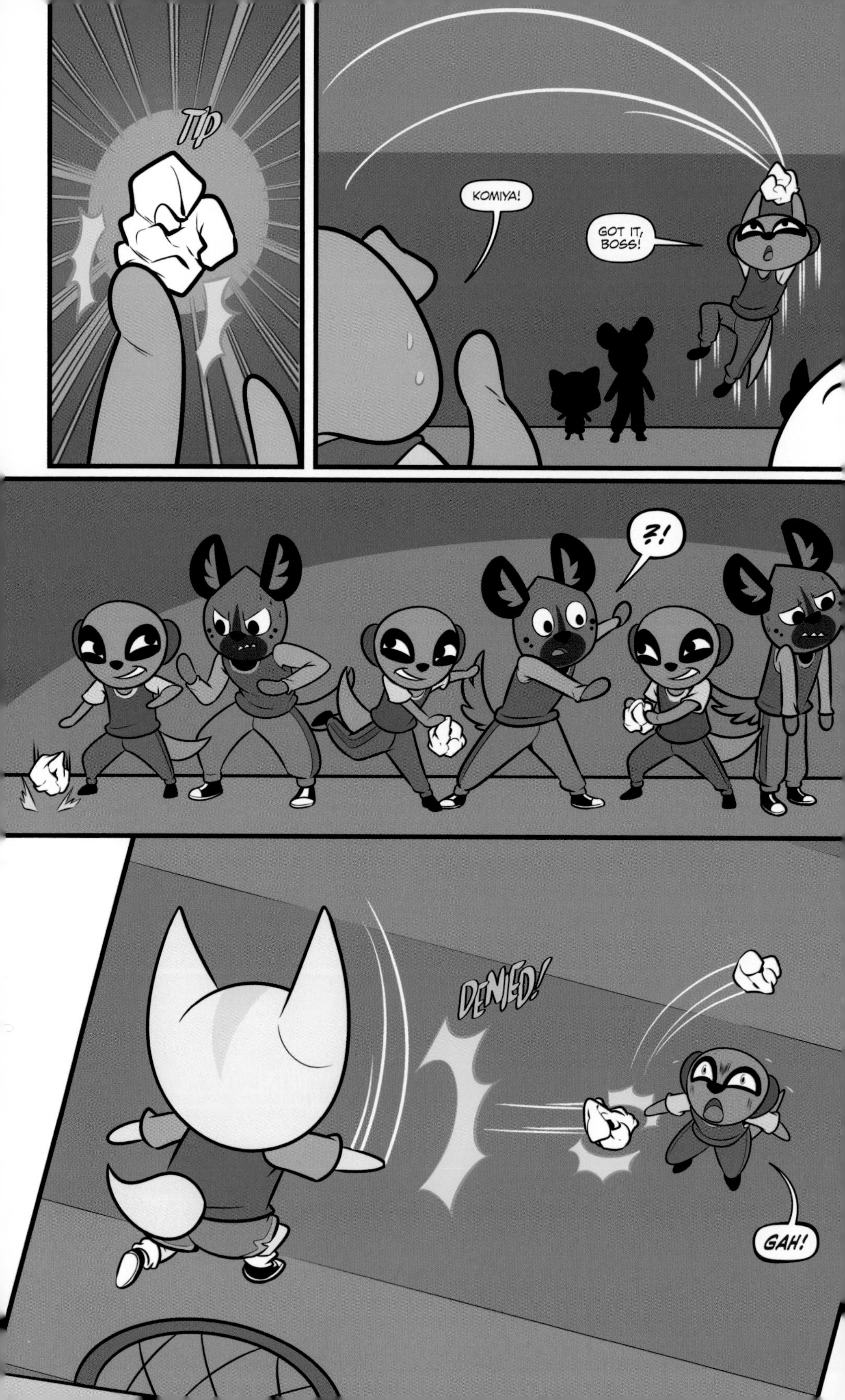
TIP
KOMIYA!
GOT IT, BOSS!
?!
DENIED!
GAH!

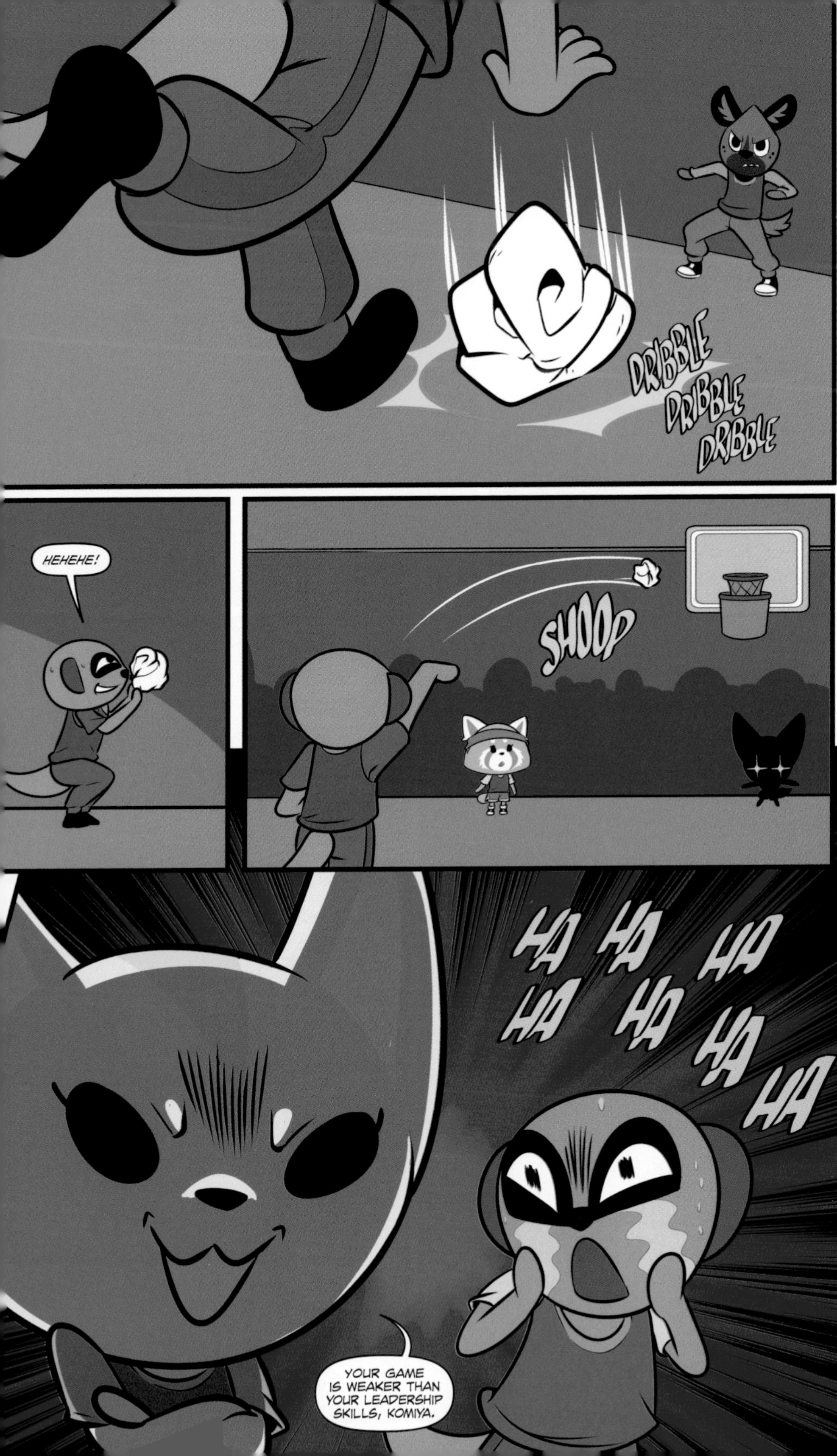
DRIBBLE
DRIBBLE
DRIBBLE
HEHEHE!
SHOOP
HA HA HA
HA HA HA HA HA
YOUR GAME IS WEAKER THAN YOUR LEADERSHIP SKILLS, KOMIYA.

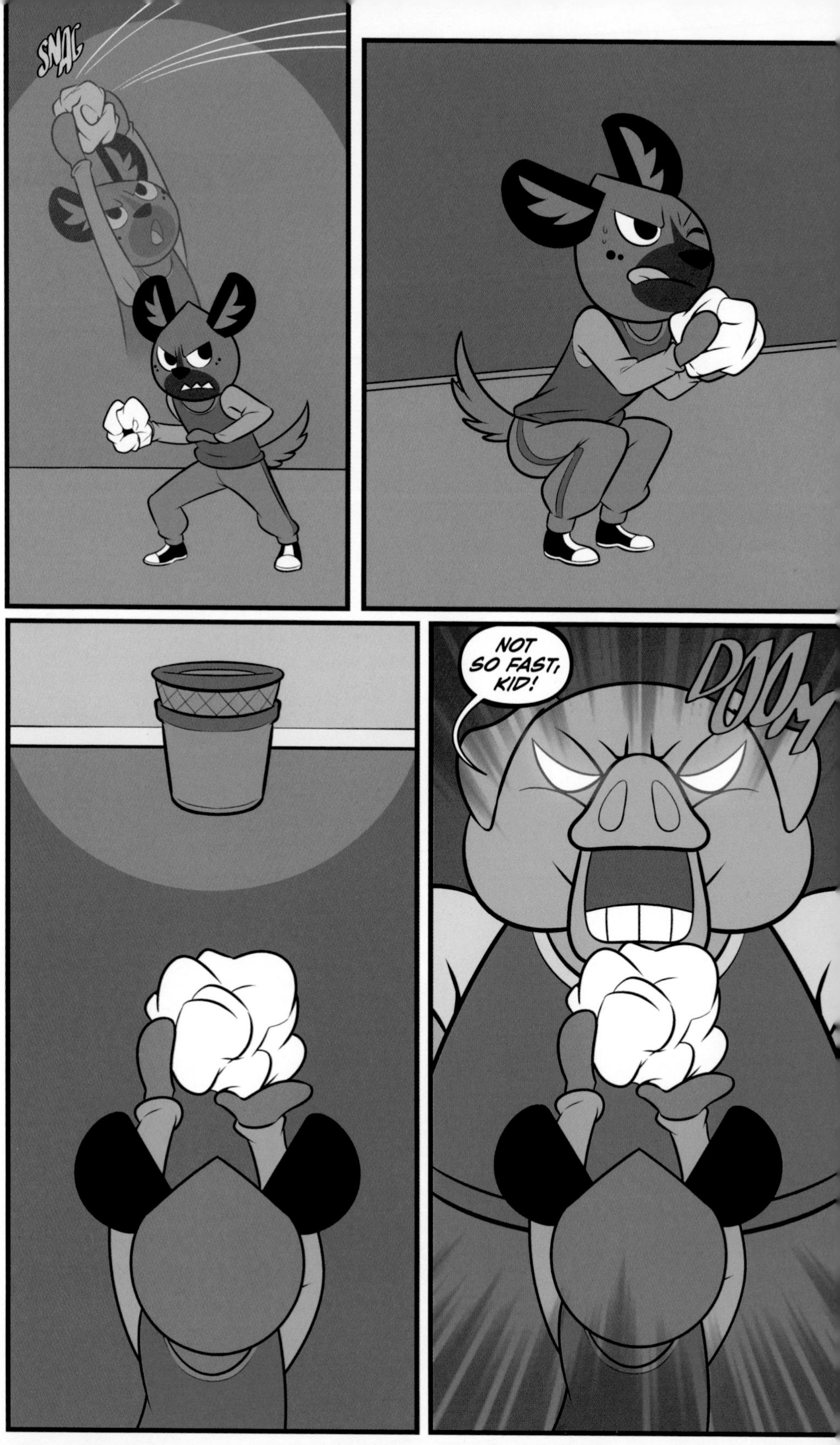
SNAG
NOT SO FAST, KID!
DOOM

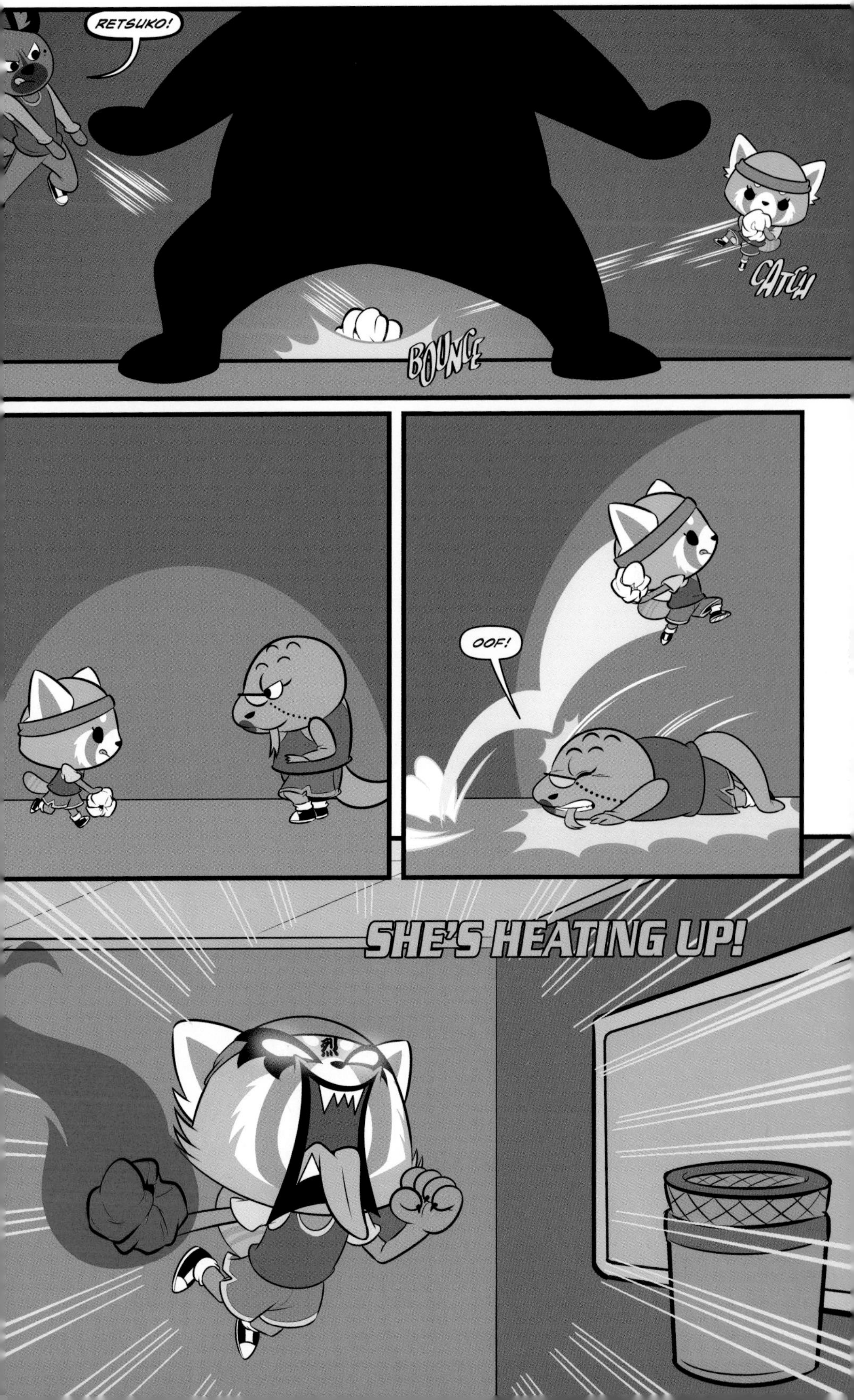
RETSUKO!
CATCH
BOUNCE
OOF!
SHE'S HEATING UP!
烈

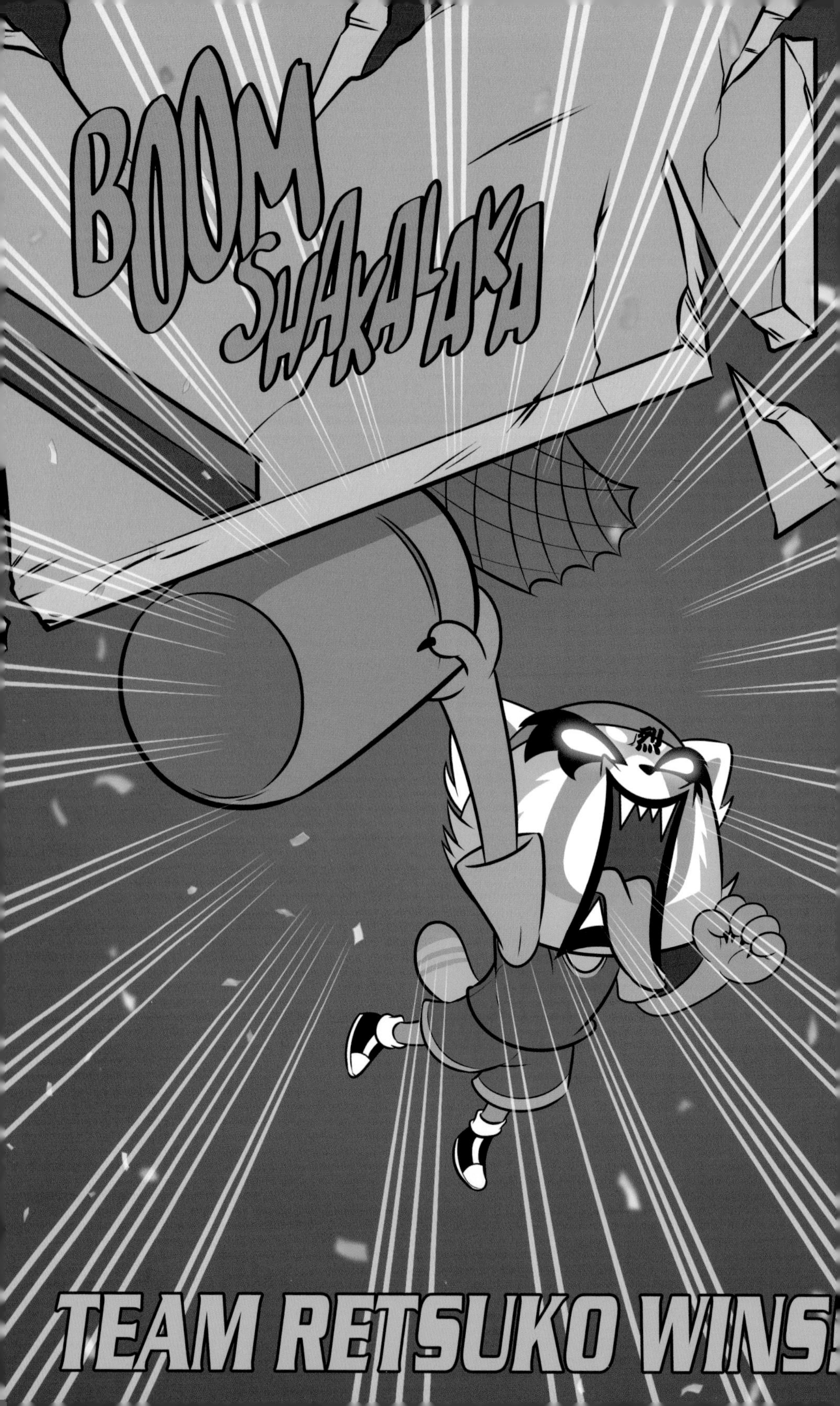
BOOM
SHAKALAKA
TEAM RETSUKO WINS!

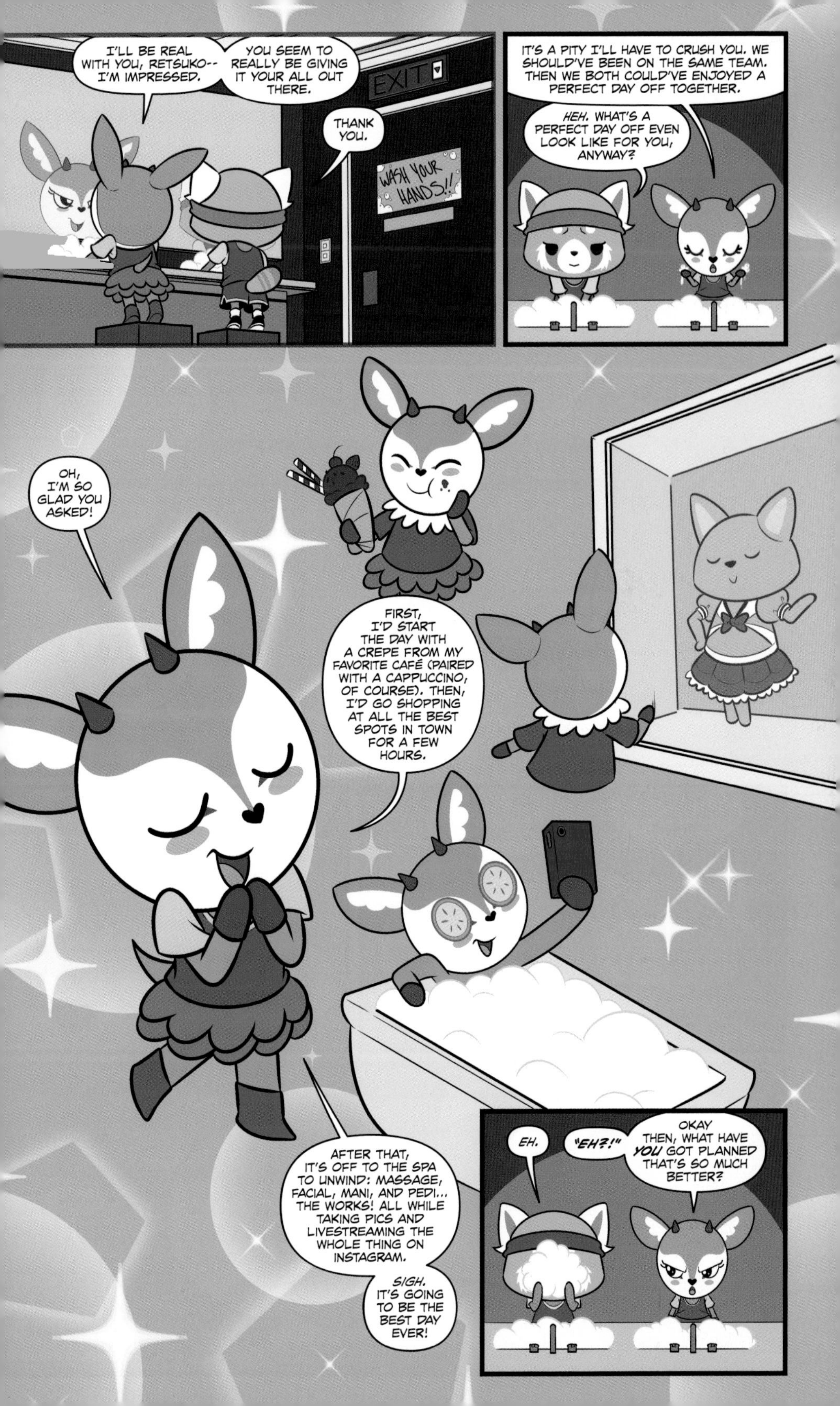

I'LL BE REAL WITH YOU, RETSUKO-- I'M IMPRESSED.
YOU SEEM TO REALLY BE GIVING IT YOUR ALL OUT THERE.
EXIT
THANK YOU.
WASH YOUR HANDS!!
IT'S A PITY I'LL HAVE TO CRUSH YOU. WE SHOULD'VE BEEN ON THE SAME TEAM. THEN WE BOTH COULD'VE ENJOYED A PERFECT DAY OFF TOGETHER.
HEH. WHAT'S A PERFECT DAY OFF EVEN LOOK LIKE FOR YOU, ANYWAY?
OH, I'M SO GLAD YOU ASKED!
FIRST, I'D START THE DAY WITH A CREPE FROM MY FAVORITE CAFÉ (PAIRED WITH A CAPPUCCINO, OF COURSE). THEN, I'D GO SHOPPING AT ALL THE BEST SPOTS IN TOWN FOR A FEW HOURS.
AFTER THAT, IT'S OFF TO THE SPA TO UNWIND: MASSAGE, FACIAL, MANI, AND PEDI... THE WORKS! ALL WHILE TAKING PICS AND LIVESTREAMING THE WHOLE THING ON INSTAGRAM.
SIGH. IT'S GOING TO BE THE BEST DAY EVER!
EH.
"EH?!"
OKAY THEN, WHAT HAVE YOU GOT PLANNED THAT'S SO MUCH BETTER?

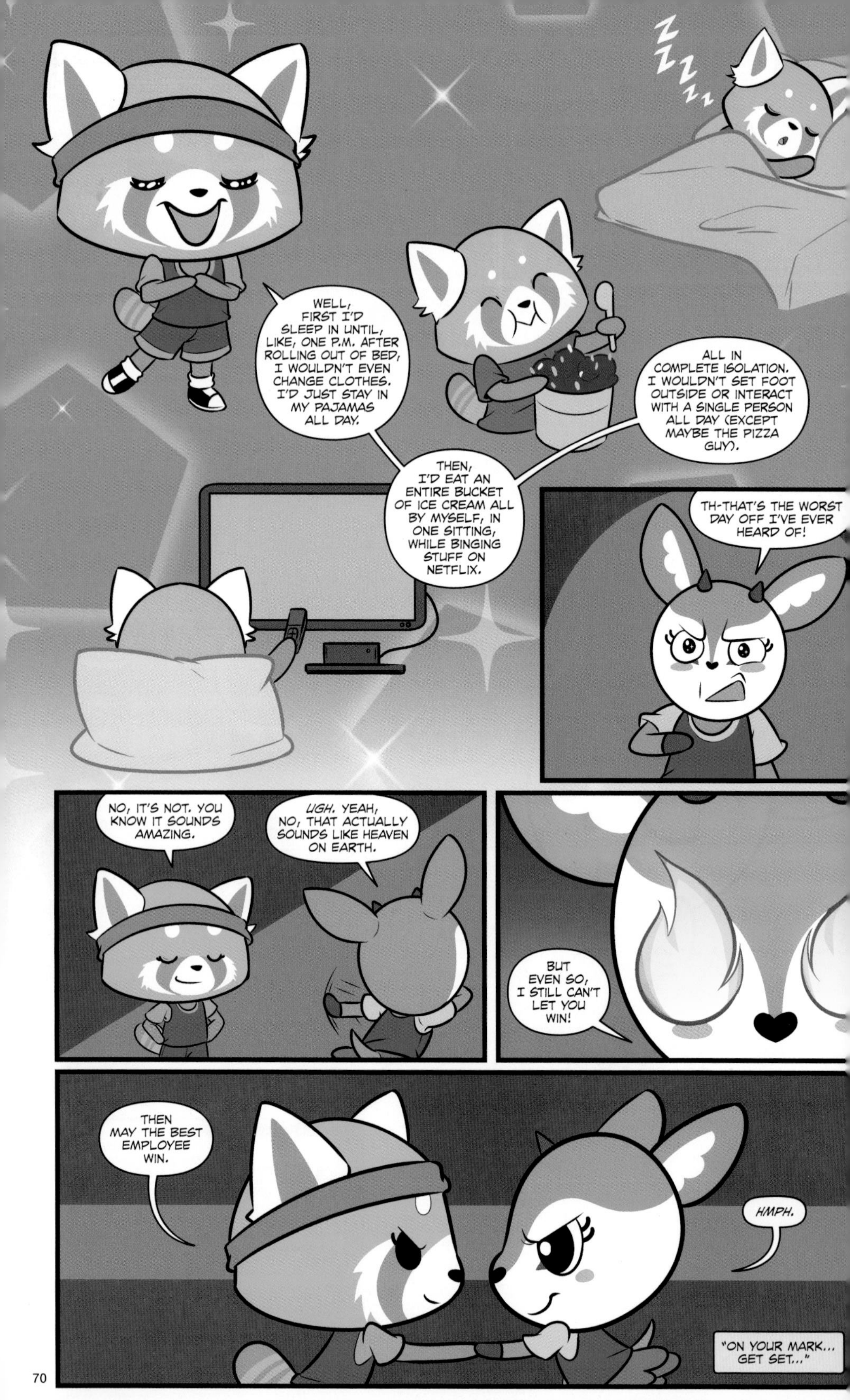
WELL, FIRST I'D SLEEP IN UNTIL, LIKE, ONE P.M. AFTER ROLLING OUT OF BED, I WOULDN'T EVEN CHANGE CLOTHES. I'D JUST STAY IN MY PAJAMAS ALL DAY.
THEN, I'D EAT AN ENTIRE BUCKET OF ICE CREAM ALL BY MYSELF, IN ONE SITTING, WHILE BINGING STUFF ON NETFLIX.
ALL IN COMPLETE ISOLATION. I WOULDN'T SET FOOT OUTSIDE OR INTERACT WITH A SINGLE PERSON ALL DAY (EXCEPT MAYBE THE PIZZA GUY).
TH-THAT'S THE WORST DAY OFF I'VE EVER HEARD OF!
NO, IT'S NOT. YOU KNOW IT SOUNDS AMAZING.
UGH. YEAH, NO, THAT ACTUALLY SOUNDS LIKE HEAVEN ON EARTH.
BUT EVEN SO, I STILL CAN'T LET YOU WIN!
THEN MAY THE BEST EMPLOYEE WIN.
HMPH.
"ON YOUR MARK... GET SET..."

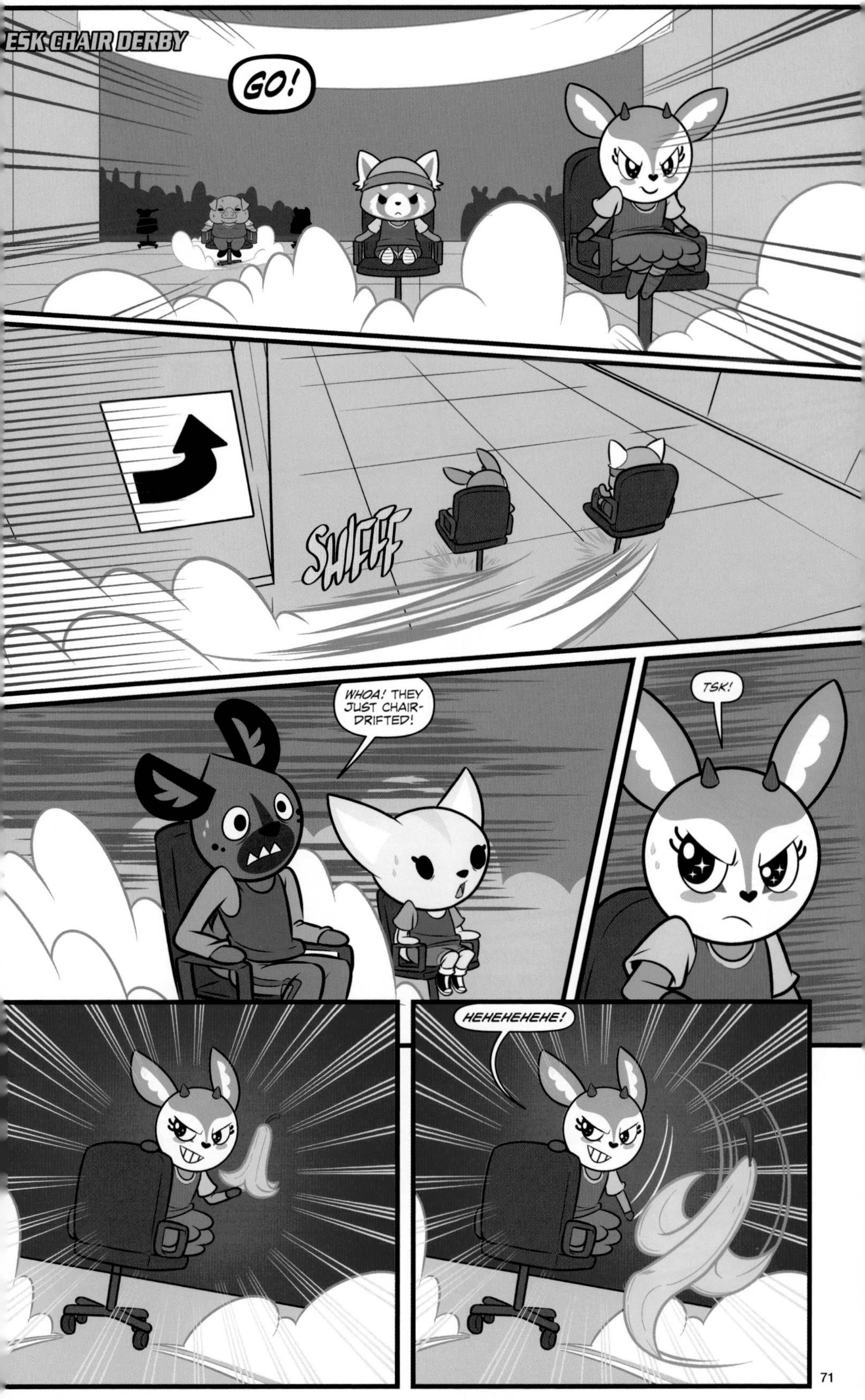
ESK CHAIR DERBY
GO!
SHFFF
WHOA! THEY JUST CHAIR-DRIFTED!
TSK!
HEHEHEHEHE!

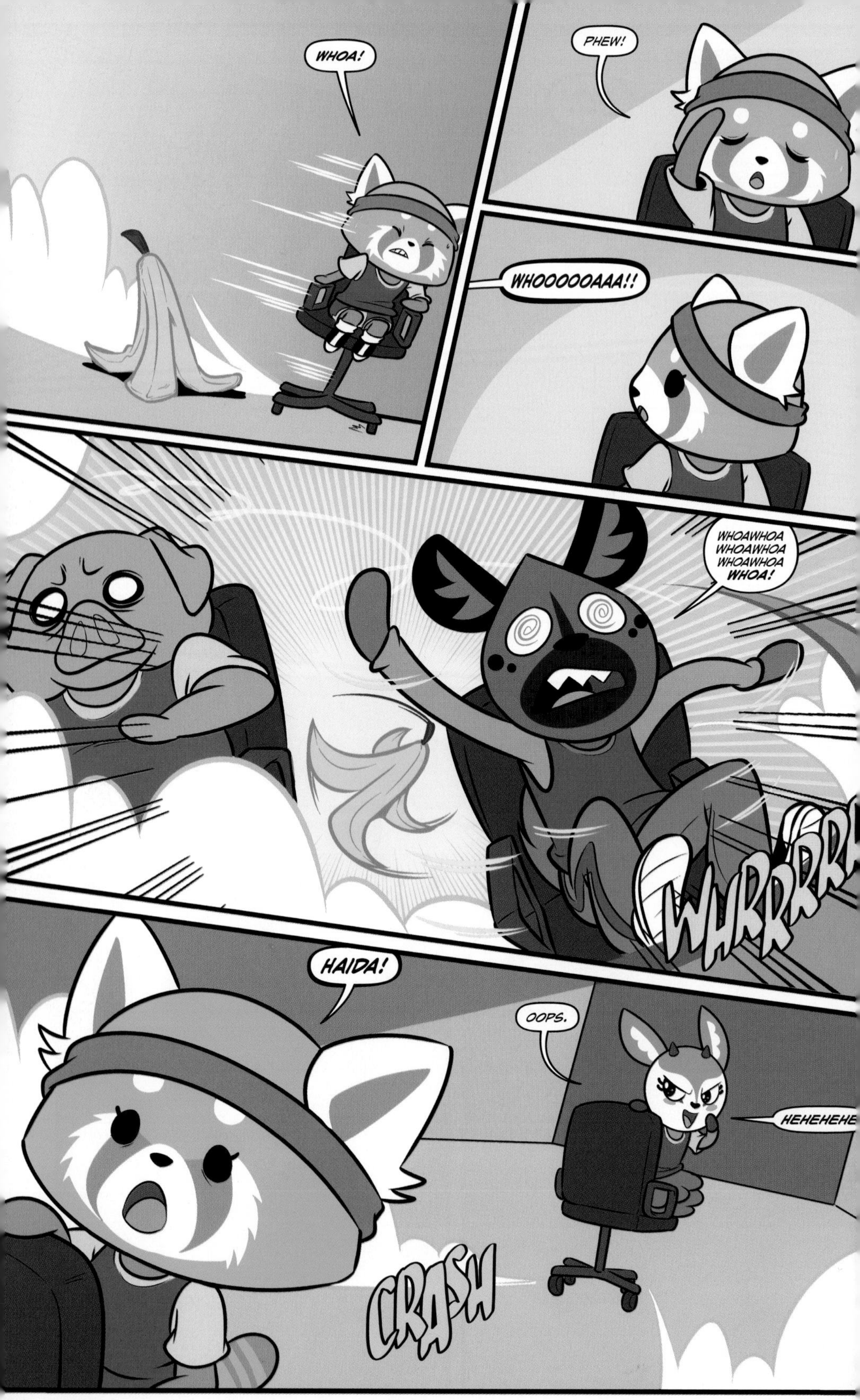
WHOA!
PHEW!
WHOOOOOAAA!!
WHOAWHOA WHOAWHOA WHOAWHOA WHOA!
WHRRRRR
HAIDA!
OOPS.
HEHEHEHE
CRASH

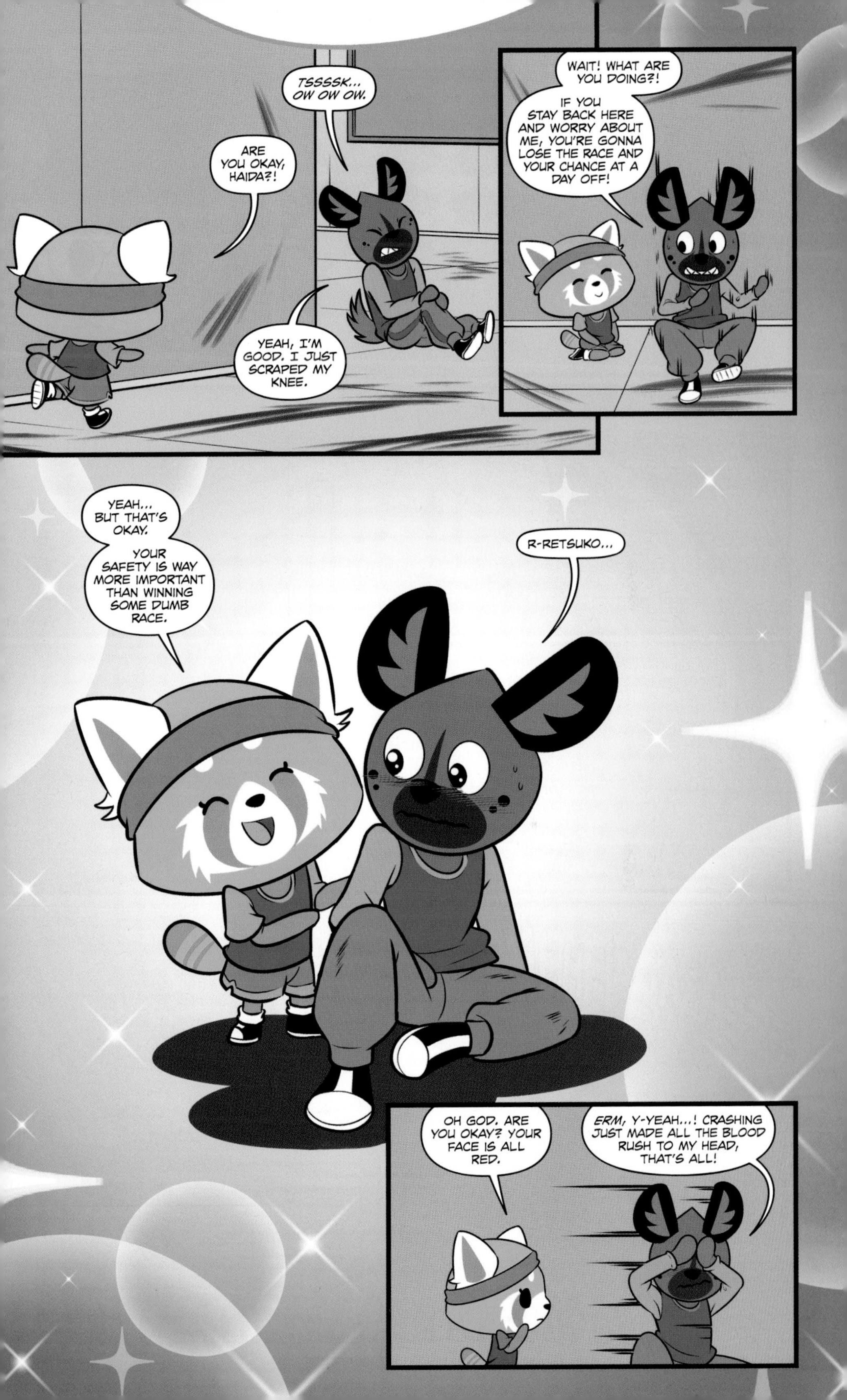
TSSSSK... OW OW OW.
ARE YOU OKAY, HAIDA?!
YEAH, I'M GOOD. I JUST SCRAPED MY KNEE.
WAIT! WHAT ARE YOU DOING?!
IF YOU STAY BACK HERE AND WORRY ABOUT ME, YOU'RE GONNA LOSE THE RACE AND YOUR CHANCE AT A DAY OFF!
YEAH... BUT THAT'S OKAY.
YOUR SAFETY IS WAY MORE IMPORTANT THAN WINNING SOME DUMB RACE.
R-RETSUKO...
OH GOD. ARE YOU OKAY? YOUR FACE IS ALL RED.
ERM, Y-YEAH...! CRASHING JUST MADE ALL THE BLOOD RUSH TO MY HEAD, THAT'S ALL!

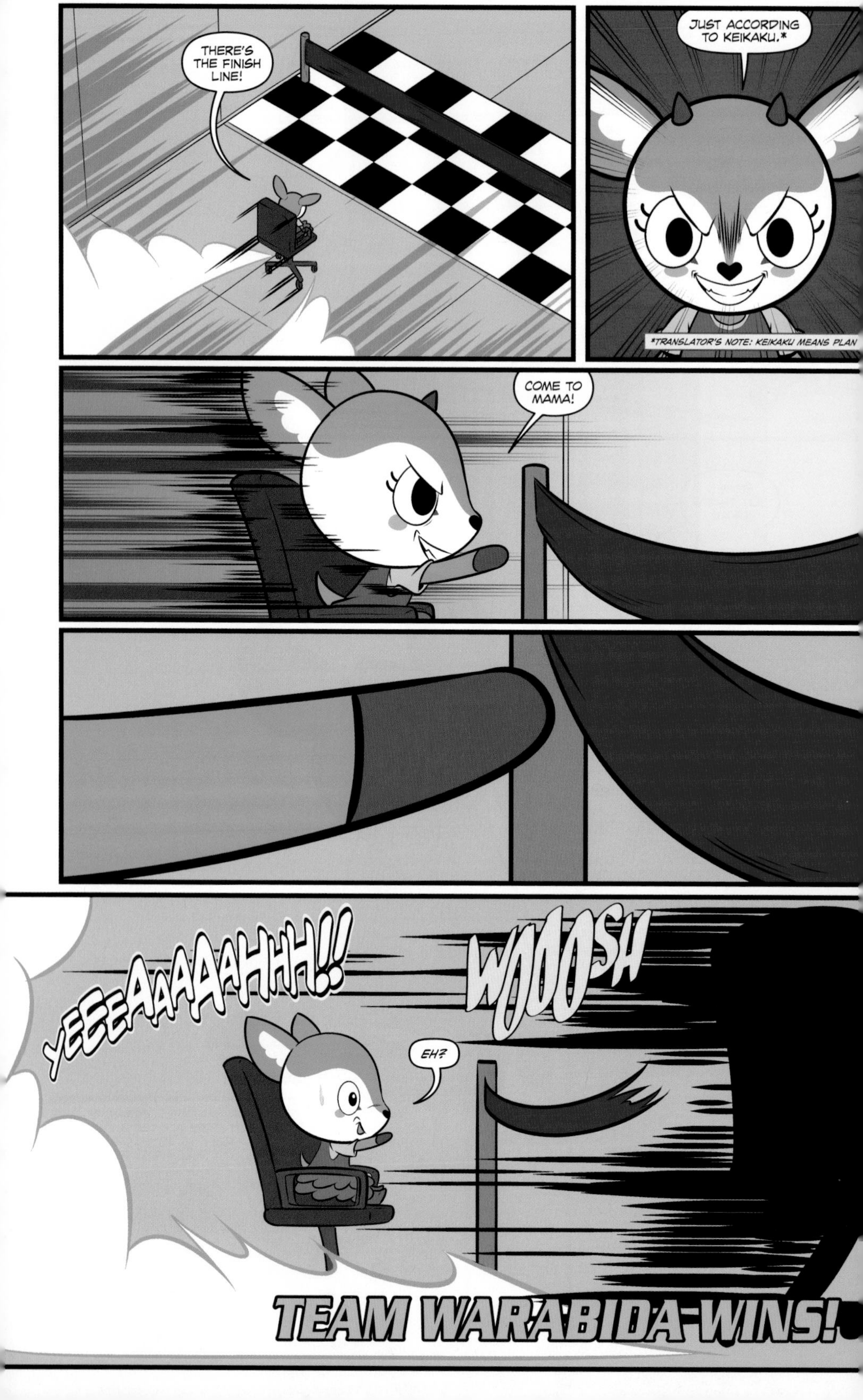

THERE'S THE FINISH LINE!
JUST ACCORDING TO KEIKAKU.*
*TRANSLATOR'S NOTE: KEIKAKU MEANS PLAN
COME TO MAMA!
YEEEAAAAAHHH!!
WOOOSH
EH?
TEAM WARABIDA WINS!

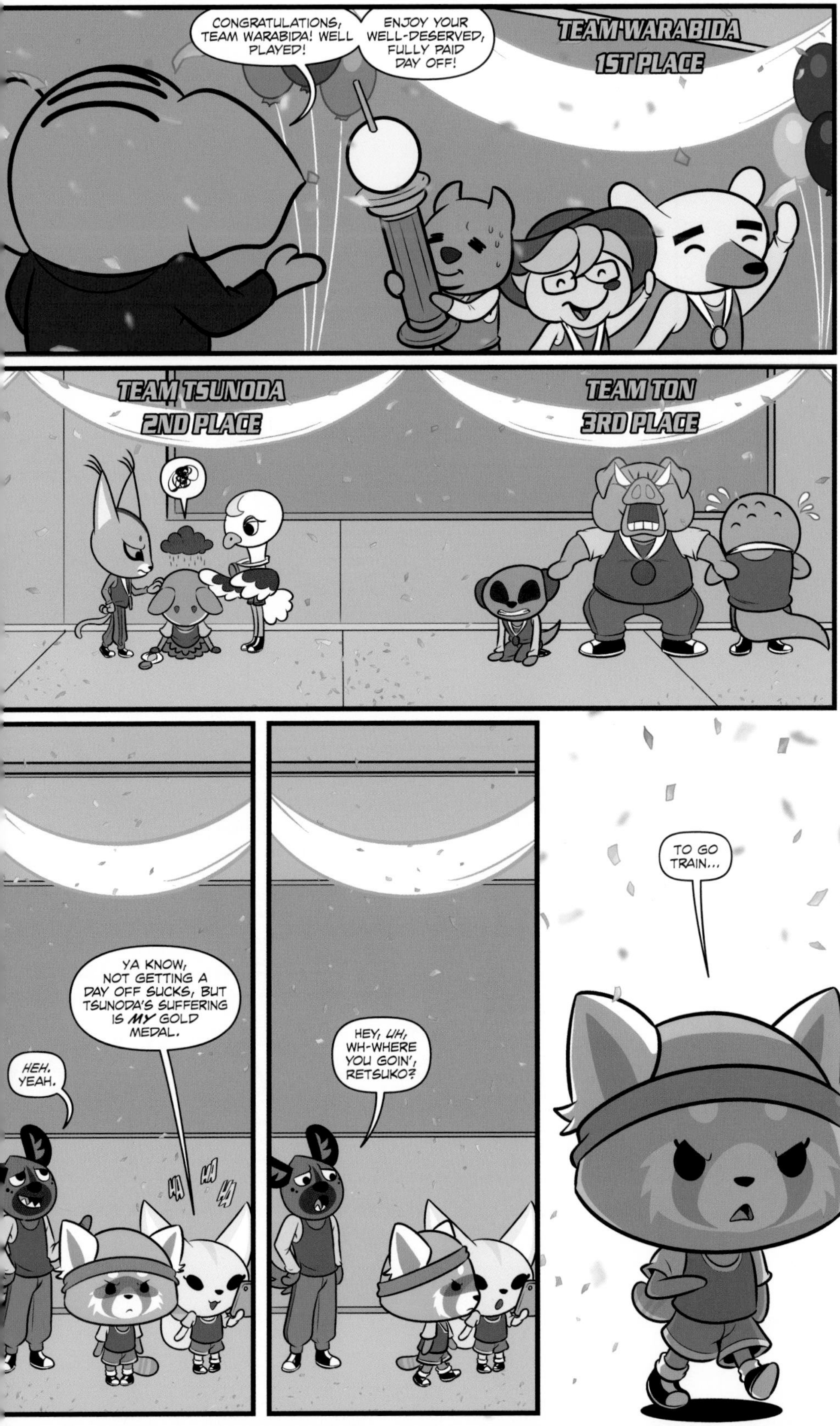
CONGRATULATIONS, TEAM WARABIDA! WELL PLAYED!
ENJOY YOUR WELL-DESERVED, FULLY PAID DAY OFF!
TEAM WARABIDA 1ST PLACE
TEAM TSUNODA 2ND PLACE
TEAM TON 3RD PLACE
HEH. YEAH.
YA KNOW, NOT GETTING A DAY OFF SUCKS, BUT TSUNODA'S SUFFERING IS MY GOLD MEDAL.
HA HA HA
HEY, UH, WH-WHERE YOU GOIN', RETSUKO?
TO GO TRAIN...

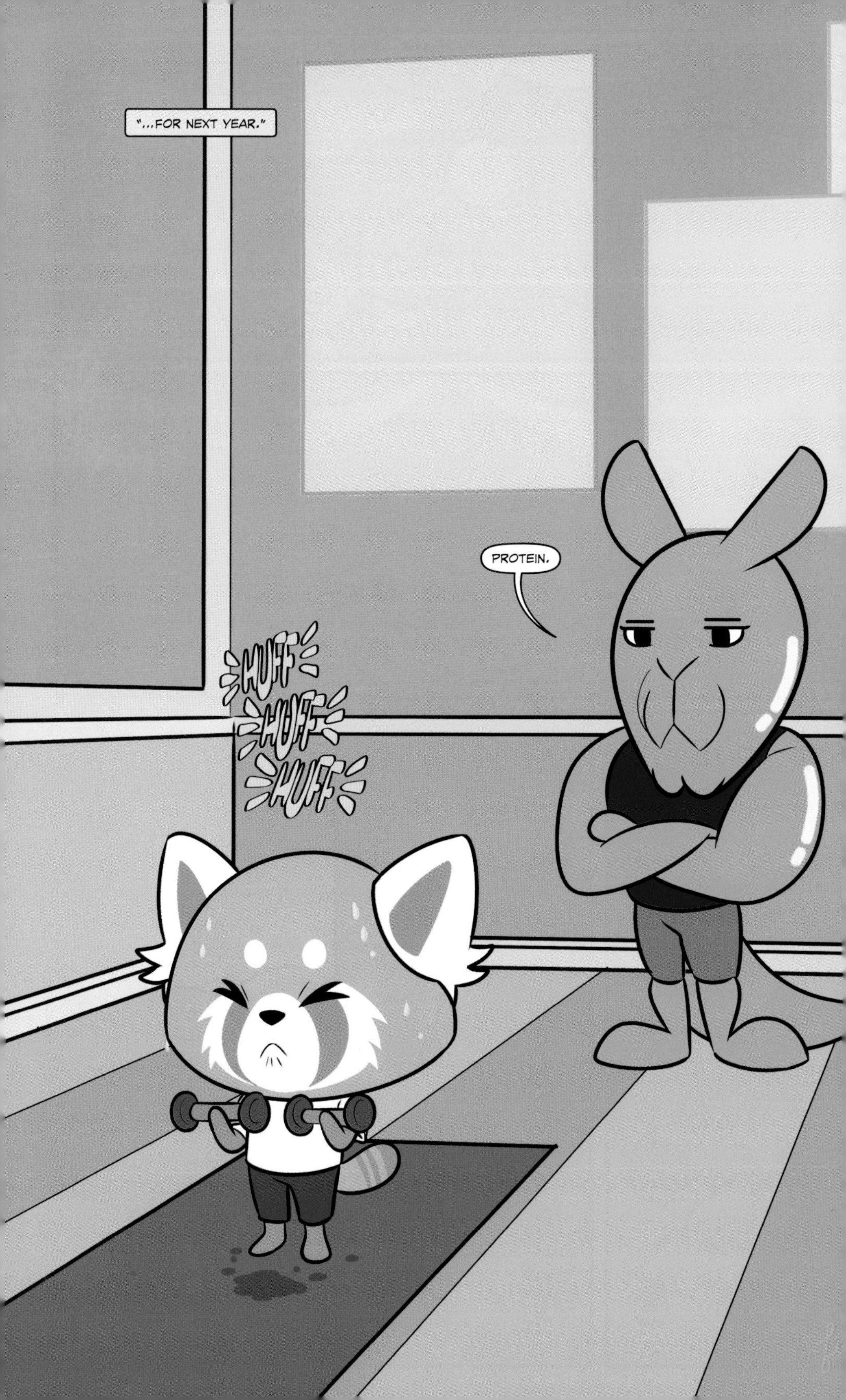
"...FOR NEXT YEAR."
PROTEIN.
HUFF
HUFF
HUFF

Aggretsuko™

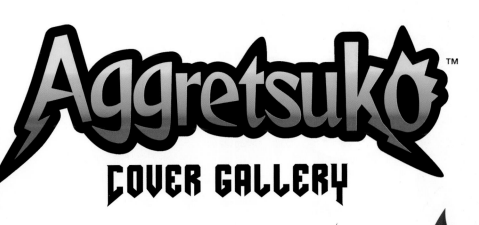

COVER GALLERY

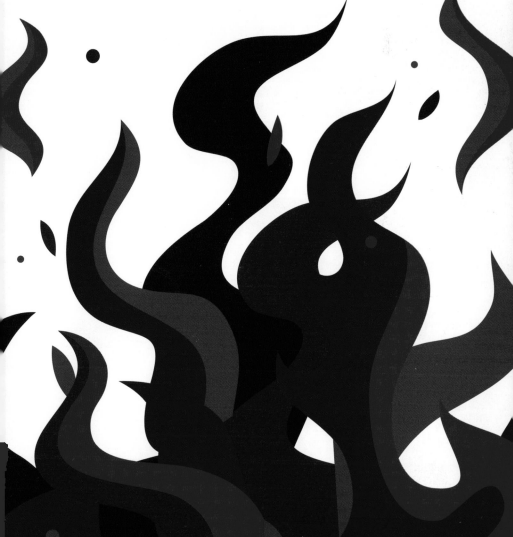

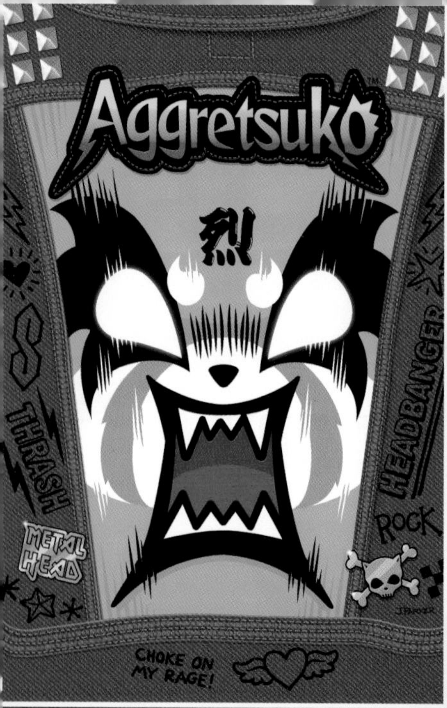
Aggretsuko
THRASH
HEADBANGER
METAL HEAD
ROCK
CHOKE ON MY RAGE!

BY JEFF PARKER

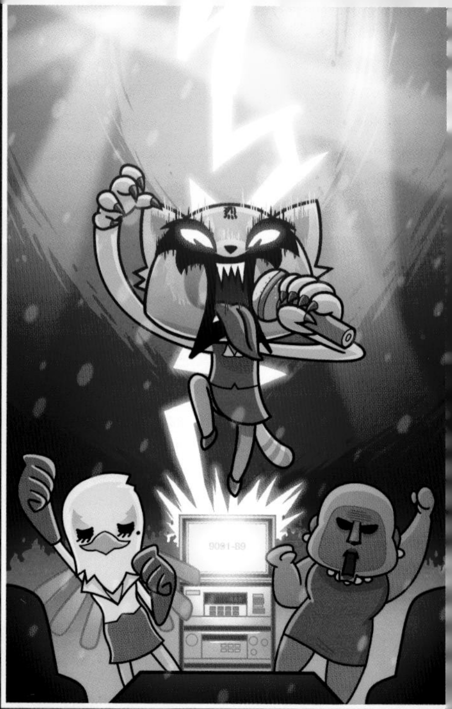

BY WARREN WUCINICH

#5 VARIANT COVER

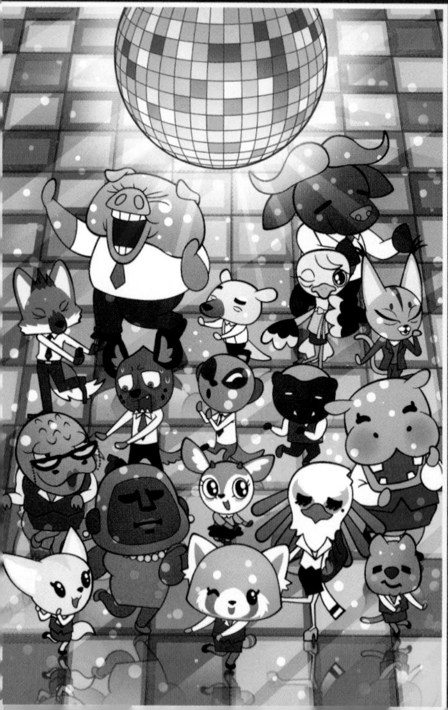

#6 VARIANT COVER

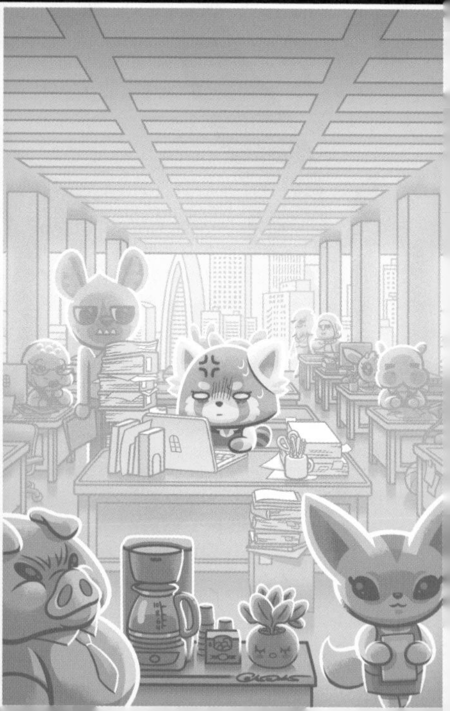

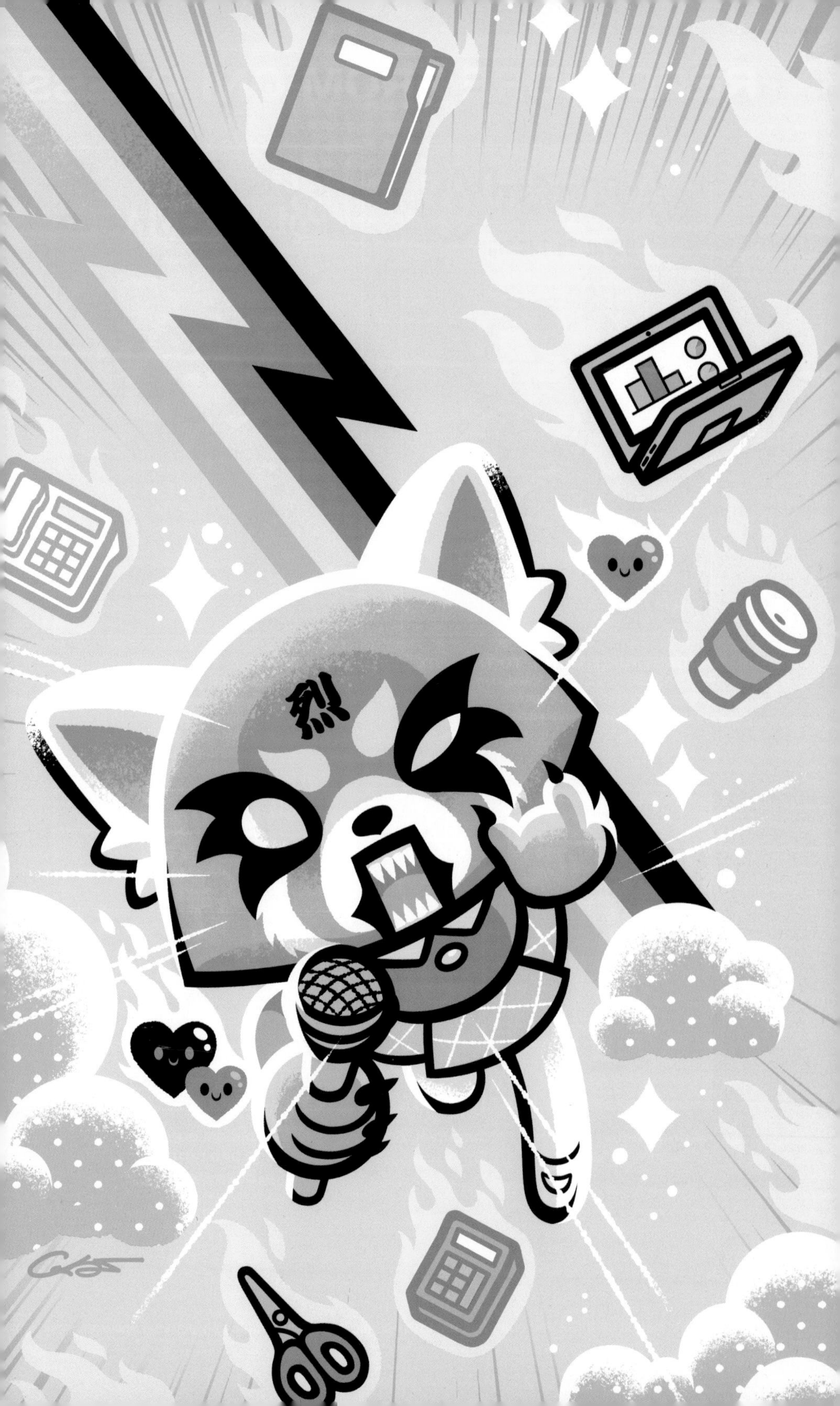
烈